Tom,

Thank you so much for the beautiful and life-like figure of a bal maiden. I shall ???? part with her — and she ?? ?? pride of place. It was such a wonderful surprise.

We have named her Thomasine after my g.g. grandmother who was a bal maiden in her youth and after her grandmother Thomasine, who was almost certainly a bal maiden when widowed, as well as being the local midwife!

With very best wishes.

Lynne

A Dangerous Place to Work!

Women and Children
of the
Devon & Cornwall
Mining Industries

by

Lynne Mayers

Lynne Mayers

2008

Blaize Bailey Books

Acknowledgements

These articles are based on papers which first appeared in the Cornwall Family History Journal between 2001 and 2006. They have since been updated, with additional images and statistics.

I am grateful to the following for their kind permission to reproduce photographs (as acknowledged in the text): Paddy Bradley, China Clay Country Park Mining and Heritage Centre, Cornwall Record Office, Bryan Earl, ICI and Mining Communications Ltd. I wish also to thank Geof Purcell for providing information on accidents at the mines and explosives works, and Tom Greeves for permission to quote from his research on the early women tin traders of Dartmoor.

Contents

Illustrations

Glossary and Abbreviations

Antimony: metal used for hardening alloys. Often used in domestic pewter, metal typeface and bells.

Bucking: method of breaking cobbed copper or lead ore down to fine granules and powder.

Bucking hammer: short handled hammer with a flat face.

Bucking plate: cast iron anvil on which copper or lead ores are bucked.

Buddle; rectangular or round frame for separating fine ores from waste.

Buddling; one of the sedimentation techniques for separating ore from waste.

Burning house: see **Calciner**.

Calciner: furnace for roasting ore to remove arsenic.

Captain: mine overseer, origin of word uncertain. In Cornish mines captains sometimes given separate areas of responsibility, i.e. underground captain, surface captain etc.

China Clay (kaolin): produced when granite begins to de-nature. Used as a filler in paper or textiles, as scouring powder, and in the manufacture of porcelain.

Cobalt: used to manufacture bright blue pigment used in paints, enamels and porcelain. Also used in alloys, especially for its magnetic properties.

Cobbing: method of breaking spalled copper or lead ore into nut sized small pieces, to separate waste.

Cobbing hammer: short handled hammer with pointed end.

Cost book: accounts ledger for mine or clay works.

Counthouse: mine office.

Croust: mid-day break (or the food eaten in this break).

Framing: see **Racking.**

Jigging: sieving fine ores under water, in order to raise light waste to the top. Initially done by hand, but eventually mechanised.

Kibble: large iron or steel bucket for bringing ore up from mine.

Kieve: vat or large barrel for washing ore.

Limp: semi-circular flat board used for skimming off waste from sedimented ore in the kieve; originally made of wood, sometimes shod with iron on the circular edge, latterly made of iron.

Manganese: used in producing chlorine based bleach and for hardening alloys.

Mundic: iron pyrites, arsenic or sulphur waste from ore dressing.

Nickel: a component of electroplating alloys, and also used in paint pigments.

Orthoclase: see **potash felspar**.

Potash felspar: used as an important constituent of good quality glass.

Racking (framing): the finest sedimentation technique to separate tin ore from waste.

Racking frame: large rectangular frame, built on the slant which is used to separate very fine tin particles from fine waste, using running water.

RCG: Royal Cornwall Gazette.

Spalling: breaking of larger rock pieces from the mine into suitable size for going on to the stamps (tin), or to the crushers or for cobbing (copper).

Spalling hammer: long handled, blunt ended hammer for breaking large lumps of rock.

Stamps: ore crushing machines for tin, originally water powered, latterly steam or electrically powered.

Tozing (tossing, towsing): settling fine tin ore in **kieves**, by knocking the side of the barrel either manually or mechanically, until a solid mass of fine ore had accumulated at the bottom.

Vanning: assessing tin content of ore by eye, using a vanning shovel and water.

WB: West Briton.

Wolfram: source of tungsten, for super-hardening steel.

Units of Money and Weight

The following Imperial Units are used in the text, as found in the original documents:

Money (£ .s. d.)

£1 = 20s (shillings) 1s = 12d (pence), 1d = 2 halfpence or 4 farthings

Weight (Ton, cwt, lb, oz.)

1 Ton = 20 cwt (hundredweight), 1 cwt = 112 lbs (pounds), 1 lb = 16 oz (ounces)

(Metric equivalent: 1 kg = approx 2.25 lbs)

Introduction

The employment of women and children across the metal mining industries of the 18th and 19th centuries has often gone unremarked and unnoticed. This is partly due to their frequent absence from the historical record and a lack of surviving mining heritage 'artefacts' which relate to their work. It is also due to a 20th century bias in interest towards mining technology, the powerful mining entrepreneurs, or to the romance of underground work. However, it seems that women and children were employed right across the mining-related industries during this time.

In the mines and quarries of Devon and Cornwall, some boys did experience the dangers of below ground work, but as many (if not more) worked at surface. This was also the place where the women and girls would be employed. They could be found in greatest numbers at the copper and tin mines, but they also dressed silver-lead, zinc, iron, manganese, antimony, china clay, slate, wolfram and uranium. In addition, the employment of women and children in the subsidiary industries seems to have been accepted as the norm. They could be found working at the smelters and in foundries, as well as at the gunpowder mills, fuse works and dynamite factories.

The late 19th century saw a continuing mechanisation, running hand-in-hand with the gradual demise of the mining industries in the Devon and Cornwall. There was also a growing public concern about the conditions under which women and children worked, resulting in restrictions on their employment, and legislation to ensure education for all. The consequence was that the employment of women and children across the mining industry was all but over by World War I.

This book is written to honour the lives of these women and children, and to acknowledge the contribution they made to the economy of the South West (and beyond) during this vital period of industrialisation. Their story is uncovered in the following chapters (compiled from a series of articles which first appeared in the Cornwall Family History Society Journal) based on census records, mining archives, newspaper reports and a very few surviving first hand accounts.

Lynne Mayers
January 2008

Chapter 1

Bal Maidens

Women and children were probably working at, or in, the metal mines or works of Cornwall and Devon from the days of antiquity. While boys almost certainly worked both at surface and below ground, the women and girls seem only to have been employed above ground (unlike their counterparts in the collieries of Wales, Scotland and the North of England).

From the late 13th century through to the mid 16th century, the metal mines came under the control of the Crown (Mines Royal) and were highly regulated. Boys were certainly employed in the early tin works, and a few records indicate that women were also working (usually with their husbands) during that time. It is also believed that females were dressing ore at the silver-lead mines at Bere Alston, Devon in the early 14th century.

From about 1720 onwards, with the introduction of mechanical pumps, ore could be more easily won from below the water table. Installation of horse whims, and then winding engines, meant that ore could be raised more efficiently and safely. These improvements required far more investment and a larger labour force, so these larger, deeper mines were no longer financed by extended families but by groups of adventurers, and, by the end of the 19th century, by mining companies.

In the early years of industrialisation, a tribute team (usually an extended family unit) would bid for a 'pitch' at the mine. This would be an agreed part of an ore-bearing lode to be worked for two months, at a pre-fixed price for any ore raised. The older boys and men, and a few of the younger boys, would be working underground. The rest of the boys and the women and girls worked on the dressing floors, where they dressed ore for their own tribute team. In later years, they were employed by the mine agent to dress any ore brought to the surface and paid at a flat rate.

Very few statistics are available for the numbers of women and girls working at the mines in the 18th century, but there were certainly 2,000 employed just at the copper mines of Cornwall, by 1800. Although only 3,250 bal maidens were recorded in the census for 1841, over 5,000 females were recorded in the mine returns of the same year for the tin, lead and copper mines of both Cornwall and West Devon. The totals for the subsequent census years seem a little more accurate and show the rough trend in female employment for the rest of the 19th century. The peak was probably in the early 1860's, when at least 6,000 were employed. (Fig. 1.)

In 1841, 700 of the bal maidens recorded were under thirteen years of age, and about 1,750 were between thirteen and eighteen years. The average age at which girls started work at the mine was ten or eleven, but some started as young as six or seven.

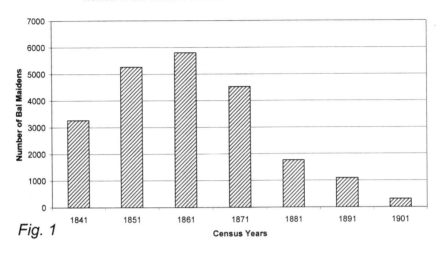

Number of Bal Maidens Recorded in the Census for Cornwall

Fig. 1

Invariably, these younger children would be those whose father had died, or where the family was in severe economic difficulty. The girls would usually continue at the mine until they were married (at about nineteen years) when their employment would cease. Some single women remained at the mines into their sixties, or even seventies. Widowed women were also employed, and might also work well into old age.

It was not uncommon for the bal maidens to walk up to 3 miles to reach the mine (some walked as far as 5 miles). Their day usually started at 7 a.m. in summer, and at dawn in winter. However at 'sampling', when the dressed ore was assayed for pricing (for about two weeks in every eight), they started at 6 a.m. They normally finished at 5 p.m. or dusk, with half an hour or an hour for lunch. At 'sampling', they may not have finished work until 8 p.m. Their working week was from Monday to Saturday lunch time, with a half day on monthly pay day. Christmas Day, Good Friday, and the

Parish Feast Day were the only full day holidays. On Midsummer's Day, the mines were given a 'Spring Clean'. Then the women and children could leave two hours early and were given 6d to spend at the Midsummer Fair. (The men received 1s 0d!). Whitsun was sometimes a half day, and occasionally the surface workers went home two hours early on Christmas Eve.

The work done by the bal maidens varied slightly with the mineral that was being dressed, but generally the women and girls were involved in:

a) hand picking ore from waste,
b) the physical breaking of ore,
c) the separation of ore by sedimentation and
d) fetching and carrying between the different processes.

Fig. 2 Engraving of Dolcoath by Allom c. 1830
Women spalling (left), cobbing (centre), picking (right) and bucking (back right)

Fig. 3 Engraving of copper mine c. 1840
Women spalling (left), cobbing two handed (centre & right) and a boy sieving? (far right)

The youngest children (up to about twelve years old) would pick and sort the ore. The young teenagers were usually involved in jigging or racking (separating and sedimentation processes). The oldest girls and women carried out the most strenuous processes: spalling, cobbing or bucking. These were the various stages in the physical breaking down of ore, using slightly different designs of hammers for the different grades. Spalling involved breaking the largest lumps of rock, cobbing the medium pieces, and the smallest pieces were reduced to granules by bucking. These older females were also employed in hand-barrowing ore between the processes. They would work in pairs, carrying 1.5 cwt of ore dry weight, which would weigh considerably more when wet (Figs. 4, 6 & 10).

Some of these processes were carried out under crude shelters, but often they were done in the open air, in all weathers (Figs. 2 & 3). The women and children worked in a noisy and dangerous environment, which was dusty in summer and muddy in winter. They wore thick long woollen dresses and shawls in winter, with woollen bandages around their legs. They wore a felt 'gook' (a bonnet which overlapped their shoulders, and protruded over the face for protection from the weather, noise and flying shards). In summer, they wore lighter clothes, and a cotton gook or (later in the 19th century) a straw hat.

Despite the appalling working conditions, the women and girls generally had better health than those working underground. However, muscular strains were common; from carrying, or the awkward bending or twisting postures required for breaking ore.

Cobbing   Jigging

Washing and Picking

Bucking and Sieving

*Fig. 4 Some of major tasks carried out by women and
children at the copper mines*

(James Henderson c. 1858)

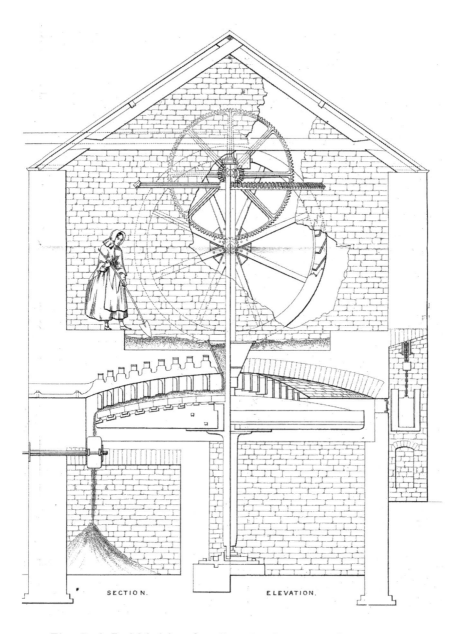

SECTION.   ELEVATION.

Fig. 5 A Bal Maiden feeding the hopper of an arsenic calciner

(James Henderson c. 1858)

10

They also suffered from rheumatoid problems where feet and legs were continually wet or damp from the ore which they were processing. Lung disease was rife, many bal maidens contracting bronchitis or tuberculosis. There were additional health hazards for those girls and women working at or near the arsenic calciners (often associated with copper or tin dressing).

Where large numbers of bal maidens were employed, the noise generated by the bucking or cobbing (especially if working under cover, in sheds) was tremendous. Also, where steam or water powered stamps were in operation, workers on the dressing floor could not hear each other speak. Thus, hearing problems would not be unusual in these women and children, and they sometimes developed their own sign language to communicate while at work.

Once at the mine, any elementary schooling ceased, although from about 1840 the girls increasingly went to Sunday School. Even so, very few were able to sign their name or read. Several commentators suggest that they also missed out on tutoring in the basic household skills, so they sometimes struggled, on marriage, with their new world of domestic duties and child care. The reality may have been very different, with so many of these young girls having to do their own share of household duties, childcare or nursing on returning home from the mine.

While serious accidents at surface were not as common as underground, bal maidens were still at risk. For example, twenty year-old Elizabeth Goyne died when a boiler exploded at United Hills Mine in February 1830, fifty-eight year-old Elizabeth Noy died when she fell from the engine house floor at Morvah Consuls in 1888, sixteen year old Eliza Jane Hall died after her leg was trapped in the winding gear at Ding Dong Mine in 1873, and ten year-old Lavinia Hellings drowned while working at the tin streams in 1875.

In the 1840s and 1850s, the youngest girls were earning 4d per day, and the eldest girls and women between 8d and 12d per day. Those under eighteen would give all their earnings to their parents. Sometimes they were allowed to keep overtime pay, depending on family circumstances. Until about 1880, bal maidens rarely earned more than enough to buy a loaf of bread per day.

Dressing tasks were slowly being mechanised from about 1830 onwards. Although women and girls were being replaced from this time, because of the continuing expansion of the industry, the number of females employed continued to increase. However, from the mid 1860s, the mining industry in Cornwall went into decline, so the numbers then began to fall. Legislation was finally enacted in 1878 banning employment of all children under ten years of age, and also the full-time working of those between ten and fourteen years old. Simultaneously, by 1880, all children up to the age of ten had to be in full time education. These changes became two more factors that influenced the economic viability of these mines, and the end of cheap full-time child labour coincided with the closure of the majority of Cornish and Devonshire mines during the 1870s and 1880s.

For female employment, there seems to have been a slight reprieve, especially in the Carn Brea area, during the 1880s and 1890s, as tin stream works expanded. Five hundred jobs for women and girls were thought to have been offered in the Red River area alone at this time. These works were collecting tin that was being lost into the river systems, from the deep mines. However, their viability was precarious, due to the huge fluctuations in the price of tin. Even they were to close all too soon, and the majority of bal maidens had been laid off by World War I.

A few mines were to continue through the war, some recruiting women especially for wartime work. This was the case at Polpuff Glass Mine (St. Dennis), Wheal Mary Ann (Menheniot) and Wheal Friendship (Mary Tavy) where the women dressed or re-dressed waste heaps for orthoclase, wolfram and arsenic respectively. Similarly, women were employed at Geevor picking belt, and dressing micaceous haematite at Great Rock Iron Mine in World War II.

However, as the mines of the south west closed, families scattered all over the world to find work. While some migrated to other mining areas in the UK, others found work in the newly opened mines of Europe, the Americas, South Africa or the Antipodes. Here, local labourers were used for the tasks that the women and girls had previously done, if machinery was not used. The women and girls of Devon and Cornwall would not be employed in numbers at the mines again, either at home or abroad. The last conventional bal maidens were laid off at Dolcoath in 1921.

All of the mining parishes of Cornwall and West Devon seem to have used female and child labour during the 18th and 19th centuries, as a matter of course. Some of the highest numbers of females employed (per head of population) were in Redruth, Camborne, Illogan, St. Agnes, Perranzabuloe and St. Just. Sadly, there is very little evidence that survives of the lives of these girls and women, as they were not considered part of the 'real' historical record. However, their contribution was vital to the economic success of the metal mining industry of the South West, especially during the 18th and 19th centuries.

Chapter 2

Bal Boys

The main period of child labour at the metal mines in Cornwall and Devon was during the 18th and 19th centuries, probably reaching a maximum in the mid 19th century. However, they had been employed long before in smaller numbers, going way back into the mists of time. Thomas Beare (the Bailiff of Blackmore) mentions boys at the tin works of Cornwall in the mid 16th century, and Carew states there were *'great numbers of boys and humane youths about washing, vanning or cleansing tin'* in the St. Agnes area in the mid 18th century. In 1841, it was estimated that there were about 4,300 boys working at the mines (1,600 under thirteen years, and 2,700 between fourteen and eighteen years). Although full-time employment of children under fourteen officially ended with the 1874 Mines Employment Act, and was subsequently reinforced with the implementation of the 1876 Education Act in 1878, it was known that some were still employed illegally, well into the 1890s. However, few young people seem to have been employed at all after about 1906.

The very first task which boys were given when they went to the mines (at about eight or nine years old) was picking or washing ore (Fig. 4). In 1841, for instance, nine year-old Richard Jeffrey was at the picking tables at Consolidated

Mines, and eleven year-old Richard Uren washed ore at Tresavean. Unlike the girls, the boys were moved on within a short time, either to work at the buddles or to work underground. The buddles were inclined rectangular frames, where waste was washed out from ore-stuff. The heavier copper, tin or lead ore would settle out at the head of the buddle, while the lighter waste was deposited lower down. To aid separation, the boys agitated the mixture with a heather broom or, in early days, by standing ankle-deep in the water and using their bare feet. Because of this, in the 17th century they were called 'lappiors' ('dancers'). They usually worked in the open and in all weathers. From 1840, the round 'Cornish Buddle' replaced the rectangular pit. Harry Thomas (ten years old) and William Rowett (thirteen years old) were buddle boys at Charlestown Mine in 1841. Harry had only been working for twelve days and simply acknowledged he *'found it rather hard as yet'*!

Jigging was a task for the slightly older boys on the dressing floor. In the early days, this involved sieving ore-stuff in boxes of water. Boys who did this for too long often 'spat blood' or developed breathing or digestive problems. By 1830, semi-automated jigging machines were being introduced, that required agitating the sieves using a long lever (Fig. 4). This work was less tiring and demanding, but only relatively so. In 1841, fourteen year-old Joseph Odgers, who had been jigging ore at Tresavean, complained of considerable pain after working all day. He hoped to be put to 'riddling' soon (sieving dressed ore). In the same year, boys at this task at Fowey Consols were paid at the highest rate of all the children on the dressing floors; 1s 1d per day.

Spalling

Packing   Tozing

Racking

Fig. 6 Some of the major tasks carried out by women and children at the tin mines

(James Henderson c. 1858)

17

Fig. 7 A boy operating a hand pump below ground
George Seymour Jnr. c. 1877. Courtesy of Mining Communications Ltd

The eldest boys could also be called on to barrow ore. Unlike the bal maidens, they used a conventional wheeled barrow. Tasks often carried out by boys, unique to the tin mines, were those of tozing and packing (Fig. 6). This involved shovelling tin-stuff into large kieves, that they had already half-filled with water. Two boys would carefully tip the sediment down the side of the kieve with a shovel, whilst a third child constantly stirred the mixture with a shovel (tozing). Once the kieve was full, one of the boys would then strike the kieve with an iron bar, fixed into the ground at one end, to settle out the sediment. This 'packing' could take between fifteen and sixty minutes, at about one hundred blows per minute. When the packing was finished, the surplus water was bailed out and the top thin layer of waste was removed with a 'limp' (a semi-circular piece of wood) for re-buddling. The sediment was shovelled out into barrows for roasting to remove any arsenic impurities. By about 1860 the packing operation had become water-powered.

Most of the work carried out by the boys at surface was open to the elements; hot and dusty in summer, and wet, cold and muddy in winter. Their working environment was described in this way in 1841:

'The work of a large proportion of the boys employed at the surface exposes them to wet and dirt; and, however wet and dirty they may be, the same clothes are worn from the time they rise in the morning until bed-time at night.' (1842 Royal Commission)

Another task allocated to quite young children (usually boys, but occasionally girls or women) was to drive the horse at the horse whim. This was at the shaft where the kibbles (buckets) of ore were raised to the surface. For instance, eleven year-old Thomas Williams, and twelve year-old Bingham Pascoe were whim drivers at mines in the Mount Whistle and Ponsanooth area, respectively, in 1861. It was both a responsible and potentially dangerous job, as the kibbles needed to be raised and lowered steadily, and there was always the danger of an overwind, or the weight of the kibble dragging people or horses back into the shaft.

From nine years old, some boys would go down the mine to work pumps (Fig. 7) or bellows for the ventilators, and to push ore wagons between the working areas and the mine shaft. In 1841, fourteen year-old James Collins worked at the bellows at Fowey Consols and complained *'his head aches for the poor air after he comes out'* as a result of noxious gas pockets where he worked. Charles Manuel (sixteen years old) had 'trammed' ore wagons for two years at Carnon Mines, but he had suffered chest pains and began to *'spit black stuff'*. He was then moved to work 'at surface' where his health improved.

By the age of fourteen, the majority of boys would be working underground at the mineral face. By the age of eighteen, they would be fully-fledged miners. At very young ages, they often took over their father's 'pitch' if their father had died or was 'in decline' (few miners were well enough to continue below ground beyond the age of forty). Jacob Waters (seventeen years old) was 'beating the borer' (drilling) at Fowey Consols, in 1841. The work was already giving him pains in the head and chest, and he was coughing 'black stuff'. Despite this, he sometimes worked a 'double stem' (i.e. two 8 hour shifts in a row). Until about 1860, when man-engines were installed, the climb into and out of the mine was by ladders, and this could take up to an hour each way.

Bad air, dust, damp, exertion, the change of temperature between the mine and surface, and the long walk home in damp clothes took their toll.

Fig. 8 Photo of St. Ives Consols Tin Mine 1863
Buddle boys (left) and racking girls (back centre & right)
Courtesy of Paddy Bradley

Boys who worked underground commonly developed lung and heart disease, and suffered digestive problems:

'In examining, even casually, a large number of miners it is impossible not to be struck with the peculiarly delicate appearance of many of them, especially the older men and of the boys and young men who have worked underground for only a short time. Instead of having the bright and clear complexions of the young people employed at surface, those who labour in the mines have a very pale sallow appearance, and this they seem to acquire even after having worked underground only for a few months'. (Kinnaird 1864)

Accidents were quite frequent. In 1841, sixteen year-old Stephen Sylvester fractured his skull when he fell 8 fathoms down a shaft at Fowey Consols, but eventually returned to work. Also in 1841, Joseph Jeffrey (seventeen years old) was struck by falling timber. He had seizures and temporary paralysis in one arm, but also returned to work. Others were less fortunate. For instance, in 1860, William Angwin (ten years old) fell down the shaft at Wheal Cock (while following his father down the ladders) and died instantly. In 1866, Benjamin Thomas (twelve years old) was killed at Balleswidden Mine by a rock fall, and in 1872 Henry Hattam (thirteen years old) fell 10 fathoms in Wheal Cole, and died later from his injuries.

In 1773, at the tender age of eight, Samuel Drew began work as a buddle boy. For his services his father was to receive three half-pence a day; but when the wages of eight weeks had accumulated in the hands of the employer, he became insolvent, and the poor boy's first earnings were lost. In the mining communities, there was no expectation that boys would do anything else but mine, and they were given home made 'toy' picks and shovels, to learn by copying their elders. Samuel obviously wanted to take to real mining very early on:

'When I was about six years old I was very ambitious of sinking a shaft. I prevailed on my brother and another boy to join me. I was captain; and having procured a board and rope, with pick and shovel, drew up what the others dug out. We must have sunk our shaft several feet when my father put an end to our mining operations.'

Despite the eagerness of these young recruits, the harsh reality of the work would come as a terrible shock. These are the words of John Harris:

'At ten years of age my father took me with him to Dolcoath Mine, to work on the surface, in assisting to dress and prepare copper ore for market. Sometimes I had to work at the keeve, sometimes at the picking-table, sometimes in the slide, sometimes on the floors, sometimes in the cobbing house and sometimes at the hutch. Sometimes I had to wheel the mineral in a barrow until the skin came off my hands and my arms were deadened with the heavy burden. Sometimes I was scorched with the sun until I almost fainted, and then I was wet with the rains of heaven so that I could scarcely put one foot before of another... After toiling away for two years, my father took me with him ... nearly two hundred fathoms under the surface... On my first descent into the mine, when I was about thirteen years age, my father went before with a rope fastened to his waist, the other end

of which was attached to my trembling self … but climbing up evening after evening, that was the tasks of tasks!'

Apart from the physical demands of the work, there was no job security for young or old. Moving from one mine (and often town) to another happened all too frequently, as described by John Prout:

'When I was eight years old I went to work at a place down from Dolcoath Tin Mine called Red River. I had to work from seven till five with an interval of half an hour for dinner, as a tin dresser for a penny a day. Then in 1852 we went to Liskeard to live, but instead of stopping in that town we went three and a half miles out to be near the mine in Menheniot Parish. There I went to work in Wheal Trelawny Mine and had sixpence a day to start with, drawing lead ore.'

Some mining boys were to rise up through the ranks, by their own hard work and abilities, to become mining engineers, captains or adventurers. Despite lowly beginnings, Samuel Drew became a famous writer, and John Harris and John Prout, poets. However, whether these 'bal boys' eventually achieved worldly fame or not, many people who had never seen a mine owed their prosperity to the sacrifice, skill and energy of this army of young men.

Chapter 3

At The Counthouse

Apart from the large number of women and girls working on the mine dressing floors and at the stamps, there were usually other females at work at the mine counthouse. These 'counthouse women' were not often mentioned, but were an important part of the total workforce, and had significant parts to play in the smooth running of the office management.

At the larger mines, the counthouse would have an office (or offices) for the manager and purser, where all bookkeeping was done, and business visitors received. In addition, there would be a large dining room, probably upstairs, where visitors and shareholders were entertained, and some had a separate 'map room'. There would also be the kitchen and various store rooms. Sometimes there was sleeping accommodation for captains on duty at night or for emergencies.

The main duties of the counthouse women and girls were to prepare the mid-day dinner each day for the agents, purser and captains at the mine. They also had to keep the counthouse rooms clean and tidy, despite the amount of dirt and dust that must have been brought in. They were also responsible for ample supplies of hot water for baths, ready for the captains and their visitors on their return from underground tours, or when they had been involved in dirty tasks at surface.

The women kept the mine officers supplied with a fresh supply of clean protective clothes. This would involve laundering of duck jackets and over-trousers (Fig. 9), which was probably done in the warm water at the engine outlet, where the local women often gathered to do their washing. The clothes were probably dried in the 'dry' or the counthouse kitchen. The counthouse women would also have the men's boots and helmets to clean after each visit underground. It seems that they were also responsible for the general upkeep and repair of these clothes, and a variety of other textile mining equipment. For instance, Mary Peak was paid 1s per month for making sacks at New Trelawney Silver and Lead Mine, in 1867.

From time to time, the counthouse women had to turn their hands to much more sombre occupations. When there were the inevitable accidents, injured miners were generally carried home. In some cases this was not possible, and so the counthouse area (probably the carpenter's shop) would become a first aid post. The counthouse women would administer what care they could, while waiting for the mine surgeon (which could take several hours). For instance, when the boiler exploded at Boiling Well Mine on 10th February 1858, it seems that the injured were carried to the counthouse area. The engineer was killed outright, and nine others were seriously scalded or burned, among them two women.

Fig. 9 A counthouse woman collecting mine officers 'underground clothes' for laundry
George Seymour Jnr. c. 1877

Courtesy of Mining Communications Ltd

It was here that Mary Webster seems to have died (shortly after the accident) and the other woman, Alice Jones died later. The dead would also sometimes be carried to the carpenter's shop, where it would be used as a temporary morgue. The bodies might remain there until the inquest the following day, if it was to be held at the mine. Thus, the counthouse staff would be involved in the preparations for both the appropriate laying out, and for the inquest itself. For instance, at Poldice Mine in March 1789, the cost book shows an entry of 6s 6d for a shroud for 'Enylew', followed by a payment to Martha Higga for 'striping him' (presumably stripping and washing his body).

The highest numbers of counthouse women found in the census returns for Cornwall were approximately 40, in 1851 and 1861. However, many were probably not recorded as they were not in full-time employment. At the smaller mines, they were just required for preparing meals for the sampling and setting days and the mine account meeting, for instance, and perhaps doing a little laundry. In general, counthouse women tended to be rather older than the bal maidens, mostly over thirty years of age. Many were widowed with young children, or single women with elderly dependants. The provision of employment was possibly seen as an act of philanthropy on the part of the mine owners. The oldest, so far found, were Ann Bade of Breage (1851) and Mary Hosking of Gwithian (1861) both of whom were seventy-two years old, and Sarah Goldsworthy of Camborne (1861), who was seventy-three. In contrast, among the youngest were twelve year-old Elizabeth Martin (1851) and thirteen year-old Evaline Shears (1891), both of Calstock.

It seems that the larger mines had at least one counthouse woman. Dolcoath had four in the 1890's: a cook, 'kitchen girl' and two maids. Betty Webb, one of the maids, remembered Christmas at the mine:

'We all looked forward to the Saturday before Christmas when Christmas dinner was eaten. On the Friday we often worked until 10 o'clock. The best tablecloths and glasses and the silver made the tables look very nice. I remember that for one Christmas dinner we cooked a boiled turkey, 3 roast geese, some chicken and roast beef and vegetables. Also we had afterwards a Christmas pudding and all kinds of fruit. There were drinks and smokes. When the men left, the women used to have their dinners. We worked hard but we enjoyed ourselves.'

Unlike most other domestic servants and housekeepers, the counthouse women were not usually resident, but were drawn from the immediate locality. For instance, Elizabeth Kitto, at Godolphin Hill, appears to have lived right next door to the counthouse. Where large mines were in remote places they might 'live in', as with Elizabeth Middleton (at Gwallon) in 1841, and Elizabeth Roskilly and Elizabeth Wittington (at Fowey Consols) in 1851. Full pay for the experienced counthouse woman seems to have been about £1 per month. This was generally more than was paid to the bal maidens for ore dressing.

Some of the later census records give an insight into other tasks that women and girls carried out at the mine office. Fanny Short (of St. Cleer), was described as a 'mine errand girl' in 1871, as were Elizabeth Gerry (at South Phoenix) in 1881 and Frances Waters (of Stray Park) in 1901. Alfreda Richards (of Gunnislake) was an office girl in a copper mine in 1881, while Beatrice Craze (of Illogan) and Margaret Rowe (of Camborne) were 'post errand girls' in 1901. Boys were occasionally employed at the counthouse as well. For instance, fourteen year-old Edward Warren of Ventonleague was a 'counting house errand boy' in 1861.

As the mines closed in Cornwall and Devon from the mid 1860s onwards, or new technology replaced manual dressing, by the beginning of the 20th century the counthouse women were often the only female employees remaining at the mine. Two of the last known 'counthouse women' were Stella Trenoweth who was employed at Geevor in the 1950s, and Sally Bradford who worked at Great Rock Iron Mine (at Hennock in Devon) until the mid 1960s.

Chapter 4

At the Clay Works

In addition to women and children working at the mines in Cornwall, they were also employed at the clay works (which produced kaolin for the porcelain, paper and textile industries). Their history is a much shorter one than at the mines, and while it is not clear when they were first working there, it was probably from about 1820, when commercial production of china clay was underway. Certainly, they were being employed by 1828. Their tasks were significantly different, however, from those women and children at the mine.

Some youngsters were employed as tool boys (fetching and carrying for the men working at the settling pits and drying pans) until old enough to work in the clay pits themselves. It seems that they were generally the 'tea boys' too! Women and girls were recruited in larger numbers for drying, cleaning and packing the china clay blocks. As with the bal maidens at the mines, most were in their late teens or early twenties, although a few were employed as young as ten years old, and others continued to work until over sixty.

Once the 'clay and water' mixture was pumped from the pit bottoms to the surface it was sequentially separated from the sand and mica impurities in settling pits, and the pure clay eventually poured into large open-air drying pans. Here it was left to dry naturally – which could take a very long time! Clay that was collected early in the year and dried over the summer months was known as the 'summer saving', and the clay that was collected in late summer and autumn and left to dry over the winter was known as the 'winter saving'. The clay would be considered ready for cutting when its water content had dropped to between 15 and 20%.

Two men would then cut the clay into twelve-inch blocks, and haul them out onto boards laid at the side of the pan. Women and girls, working in pairs, would then carry the blocks away on these boards to the dressing yards. Alternatively, if good weather was anticipated, they would carry them out onto the hillside and lay them out in rows to dry. At Goonvean, between 1833 and 1836, it seems that contractors employing groups of women to 'take out clay' were paid '1d per yard' (probably a yard laid out over a given width). These women mostly worked in groups of four to eight, and in some cases the subcontractors also appear to be women, as in the case of Ann Brook and Kittey Grigg. When the clay was dry, the blocks all had to be brought back in to be stacked in the dressing yards. In 1852, a visitor described the scene when the sun pans were being emptied:

'The scene was animated by the constant passage of women with white bonnets, aprons and sleeves carrying cubes of clay for placing beneath reeders, in sheds or in their hundreds on drying grounds on the surrounding hills, by the comings and goings of heavy sand wagons, the creak of pump and horse whim and the sound and motion of countless water-engines about their endless tasks'.

Fig. 10 Three women dressing clay
Courtesy of China Clay Country Park Mining and Heritage Centre

33

Fig. 11 Carloggas Clay Works c. 1907
A re-created scene to illustrate the work of clay dressers

Courtesy of China Clay Country Park Mining and Heritage Centre

In poorer weather, the clay was carried straight to the yards by the women and girls, to be stacked into towers about six feet high, and with the blocks laid in such a way as to allow good air circulation. They then covered the tops of the towers with thatched hurdles (called reeders) for protection from the rain.

Eventually, when the blocks were completely dry and ready to be sold, they were cleaned and packed by the women and girls (Figs. 10 & 11). Cleaning took place in the open air at a slatted trestle table, and presumably only in dry weather (unlike the ore dressing at the mines). Sometimes, there was a reed hurdle erected for protection from the sun or wind. The women would work standing, in pairs or fours at each table, cleaning the china clay blocks with a triangular iron or steel scraper. They had to remove any algae, staining or sand grains adhering to the blocks. One writer describes them cleaning blocks by placing them on a board braced between themselves and the table, and scraping them with a two handed scraper that sounds similar to a spoke-shave (but no photographs or illustrations of these have been found). The women who cleaned the blocks were paid by the day (8d at Lower Ninestones Pit, in 1828) or by the number of tons cleaned (4 or 5d at Goonvean, in 1835). Finally, those who packed the cleaned blocks into wooden casks ready for transporting were also paid by the ton (6d at Goonvean, in 1835). By the end of the 19th century, the daily wage had risen in line with the amount the bal maidens were paid at the mines, which was one shilling per day.

From a few surviving photographs of females at the clay works, we can see that they wore much the same as their counterparts at the mine dressing floors. As it seems that they did not work in the real extremes of weather or bad conditions their clothing is modified accordingly. In summer, they wore long cotton skirts, long-sleeved cotton blouses (sometimes with protective over-sleeves) and the cotton gook. In cooler weather, they wore woollen skirts, shawls and warmer padded hats. They appear to wear rather lighter shoes than the bal maidens, but presumably they only worked when it was relatively dry underfoot, and they were not required to clamber over or between heaps of ore and rubble in the course of their work. Surprisingly, they are always shown working bare-handed.

In the first half of the 19th century, their working day was shorter than the ore dressers, being from 8 a.m. until 5 p.m. (but sometimes working into the night). After about 1850, their hours were increased to be on a par, i.e. starting at 7 a.m.. However, it seems that this employment, unlike most women and girls at the mines, was not full-time, but was both seasonal and weather dependent. With little to do over the winter months, they would be needed during the first reliably warm dry spells of the year, to move the blocks out for drying onto the hills or into the dressing yards. They would be needed again to bring the blocks in when they were dry, and then to clean the blocks when they were ready for sale. In this way, they must have been taken on and laid off at very short notice. Surviving Cost Books (account books) indicate the irregular nature of their employment, with months when few or no women were employed at all (especially between November and February). The Clay Works employed comparatively few 'maidens' compared with the metalliferous mines of the same period. The largest numbers employed seem to be for the laying out of the clay, but probably no more than twenty to thirty at one time. The scraping and packing appears to have been done by much smaller numbers, in teams probably not more than about six or eight. In some cases, 'gangs' of women and girls were moved around from one clay works to another (where they were under the same management) as required. Also, the women seem to have presented themselves for work at different clay works during any one year, as the opportunity arose.

Because of their part-time working, it may be that the clay maidens are even more under-recorded in the census than their counterparts at the mines. However, there were probably never more than a few hundred employed in Cornwall at any one time. From about 1850 onwards, some of the works began to install indoor 'pan dries', heated by coal-fired furnaces, which dried the clay much more quickly and effectively, and dried it clean. This meant it could be packed directly into casks or wagons ready for transport. Women and girls, then, were no longer required to lay out blocks in the fields, stack them in the reeders, nor clean them prior to sale.

There were 37 female clay workers recorded in the census in 1841, which rose to 140 in 1861. However, by 1871 this figure had fallen to 60. It is not clear when the last clay maidens were laid off; although, some smaller works (such as Carloggas) continued to use the 'sun dry' method until they closed in the early 20th century. Only eight clay 'maidens' appear in the census for 1891 and then, finally, only one in 1901. While most of these maidens were employed in the St. Austell area, a few were also employed at the clay works in the Nancledra, and Tresowes areas of West Cornwall, and at Lee Moor on the south fringe of Dartmoor.

As with the mines, some women and girls were called back into employment at the clay pits to replace the men who had volunteered for war service. During the First World War teams of women worked a shift system at the monitors (hoses) washing out clay from the pit bottoms. This was known to have happened both at Rocks and Gothers China Clay Works. Women were also employed bagging up ground china clay at Little Treviscoe in WWI, and at Great Treverbyn Mill in WWII.

Chapter 5

Slate Dressers and Packers

The largest complex of slate quarries in the South West is at Delabole, on the north coast of Cornwall. Slates were probably first extracted there about six hundred years ago, and are still being extracted today. High quality slates have been exported from there to all over the world. It seems that, by the 18th century, tribute teams were employed, under much the same system as at the Cornish mines, and although the employment of females is not recorded as such at this time, they may well have contributed to the work of the these teams. Certainly, young boys were at work on the dressing floors at this time.

The following description, from 1850, gives us an inkling of the environment in which these women and children lived and worked:

'Two villages owe their origin to the Delabole quarries, Pengelly and Medrose. These quarries present one of the most astonishing and animated scenes imaginable. The traveller suddenly beholds 3 enormous pits, excavated by the uninterrupted labour of centuries, slowly encroaching on the domain of the farmer. Upon the edge of each quarry is the Papote Head or platform from which guide chains are stretched like the shrouds of a ship to pit bottom. The slate,

after blasting, is placed on a truck, which being attached to a wheel traversing a guide chain, is drawn up to the Papote head by steam engine. Moveable hatches are run out 14 ft over the face on to which the truck lands and is then drawn away by horses to the workshops.'

Turner, writing in 1854, mentions 'cullers', or 'hullah bobbers', searching the waste heaps on the dressing floors for good slate. These were usually young boys, who were able to make a living from dressing the scraps. In early days, dressers would probably be working out in the open air, or in crudely erected sheds made from rejected slate. These sheds were only open at the front, giving more protection from the weather than their counterparts in the copper, lead and tin mines. While the exact nature of the work done by the women and girls is not clear, they were described as being *'of equal ability to the men'*.

When Jenkin describes the work on the dressing floors in 1888, he mentions boys being responsible for dressing 'scantle' (mixed small-sized slate). This was sold for roofing outbuildings, such as mine engines and boiler houses. Although there is no evidence of women or girls working at the quarry at Delabole beyond about 1855, these tasks, ascribed latterly to boys, may also have been those done by women and older girls at an earlier date.

While Delabole has always been the largest in Cornwall, there have been a great number of slate quarries in the county, many also on the north coast. One of only two references (so far found) of females employed at a slate quarry other than Delabole, is from the 1851 census for

Tintagel. Here, a thirty-nine year-old widow and her two young sons are all described as 'sorting slate'. They may have been 'cullers' or 'hullah bobbers,' as mentioned earlier.

Dressed slates were taken to the yard by 'pitchers', who carried them in V-shaped hods on their backs. Slates were then stacked in rows of one hundred dozen (15 slates to a dozen, to allow for breakages) with each five dozen marked by a slate turned on edge. The younger girls employed at the slate quarries were probably involved in this stacking and counting of the slates. Local custom has it that women and girls were involved in this work at the Carnclaze Slate Quarries, near St. Neot.

As well as possibly dressing slate, women were also involved in its transport. Around 1836, one of the Delabole companies bought six donkeys to carry the slates to, the 'slate depot'. They then employed a woman to drive them. Apparently this method of transport was very successful, and most of the carriage was done in this way until about 1850, when bullock carts were used instead.

According to the 1842 Mining Employment Commission, in 1841 there were nine girls and twenty one boys under the age of thirteen years, and seventeen girls and thirty-four boys between the ages of thirteen and eighteen working at Delabole. No figures were recorded for adult female employment. The children were usually hired as daily labourers, with their wages ranging from 2s to 5s per week, depending on age. A deduction was made from their earnings for their tools.

Most of our other information about the employment of women and children at the slate quarries comes from the census. The 1851 census for the parish of St. Teath records twenty-six quarry women or girls, and thirty-nine quarry boys. There are also records of a sixty year-old widow working at a slate quarry in St. Clether and twelve boys at a slate quarry in Tintagel, for the same year. By 1861, there were nearly one hundred boys at Delabole and fifteen boys at Tintagel, but no longer any females recorded at either. By 1871, there were sixty and thirty-five boys at Delabole and Tintagel, respectively.

Despite no longer working at the quarries themselves, women continued to be employed on the north coast of Cornwall for packing slates into ships for export. Because of the lack of deep water harbours in easy reach of Delabole or the other slate quarries on the north coast of Cornwall, small ships were run up on suitable beaches at high tide. They were deftly and quickly loaded as the tide came in so that they could sail off the beach, fully laden, at the subsequent tide. This is known to have happened at Port Gaverne and at Tintagel, and may have happened elsewhere as well (Fig. 12). At Port Gaverne, there were often as many as six ships waiting to be loaded, at anchor in the bay.

Because the opportunity to load was strictly in accordance with the tide, teams of women and girls were 'on call' at short notice, for any time of day or night. For instance, when the office at Delabole Quarry received a signal that a ship was ready to come in for loading, they would send a street crier to call out the employees from the Port Isaac area.

Fig. 12   The beach at Tintagel, by Finden 1842
Showing the slate-lowering hoist

Fig. 13 Slate Packers at Port Gaverne, c. 1880
Courtesy of the Cornwall Record Office (AD/255/62)

Fifty or more wagons would be loaded as quickly as possible at the quarry. They then made the journey of about five miles from Delabole down to Port Gaverne, each drawn by teams of two or three horses, and supervised by two men.

Meanwhile, the women would already be on board the vessel (Fig. 13). Two women would stand on the loading platform and receive the very large, heavy slates from the men below. Another eight or ten women would be on the main deck, passing the slates in a human chain down to the hold. Here, they were deftly stowed by more women. From an advertisement for the Camel Quarry, in 1856, it appears that local materials such as rushes and moss were used for packing. In a photo of 1889, two wagons are drawn up beside the ship. The nearer one, when empty, is used as a platform from which the men work to unload the full wagon on the outside. A similar, but more distant view, of slate packing at Tintagel survives, which shows the actual packing in progress.

The age range of the women who worked as slate packers appears to have been from about seventeen to fifty years old. In the 1880s, these women were paid 4d per tide and were employed by the ship's captain, not by the slate companies. Apparently, the teams were fiercely competitive, seeing who could load the fastest. The work was described in this way:

'The task, straightforward but arduous, demanded little or no skill, yet, few could comply with its strenuous nature ... not only was this work hard, but the hours of commencement often most undesirable'.

To describe the task as requiring no skill seems somewhat harsh. With the weights of the slates involved, great care would be needed to prevent injury either to oneself or to others in the team. Also, there must have been considerable skill in packing the slates without breakages, and to ensure their safe passage even through the worst of storms. It is worth noting that, although the slates were loaded and packed onto waggons by men and boys at the quarry, the more delicate and careful job of stowing for shipment was allocated to women.

When the loading was being done at night, the women worked by the light of huge lanterns hung from the masts and rigging. The photos, taken in bright, dry weather, show the women in their full-length skirts, wearing protective aprons and over-sleeves, but seemingly no gloves! From the ship's accounts, it seems that some food and drink was provided for the slate packers, when working late. When the last slates were stowed, then the women could go home, while the ships slipped safely out of the harbour at the height of the tide, and on to their various destinations.

Chapter 6

Smelters, Foundries and Sampling Offices

Apart from working at the mines, clay works and slate quarries in Cornwall and Devon, women and children were to be found working in a range of other related industries. In some cases this continued right up to the turn of the 19th century. This included the lead and tin smelters, various foundries, as well as at the sampling or assay offices of the larger mines.

Lead Smelters

The very earliest records of women and children working at smelters in Cornwall date from the beginning 14th century, when lead-silver ore was discovered on the east bank of the Tamar (near Bere Alston). This ore had a very high silver content, and was vital for the new coinage. The ore was raised and dressed on site, and then taken by boat over the river to Calstock for smelting (Fig. 14) (Pb1). These Mines Royal employed about 700 people, including women and children.

The traditional 'bole' furnace did not fully separate all the lead and silver from the waste, some being left in the black slag. This slag was crushed and washed, and then re-smelted at a higher temperature in an ore furnace to retrieve some more of the valuable minerals. Women and children were responsible for washing this slag ready for the second smelting. It seems this washing was done in the watercourse next to the boles and furnaces at Davypulle.

No details are given of the method of washing, but each washer had an 'assistant' or 'servant'. This is reminiscent of the system still in use in Derbyshire in the 16th and 17th centuries. As it is thought that miners from that area had been recruited to the Devon mines in the 14th century, they may have brought these methods with them. The women would probably wash the slag in a sieve or grading pan. Their assistants would carry away the cleaned residue ready for re-smelting, and would also re-fill the sieves for them. The women and children were sometimes paid for washing and sieving tan bark ash, which was used in the refining process for separating silver from lead.

These 'pairs' (washer and assistant) worked up to six days a week, and, during the summer months of 1306 four or five pairs were normally at work. Agnes Oppenhulle seems to have been the first woman employed, in May 1302. Mattillid de Suchetone initially began work as an 'assistant', but eventually was employed in her own right. Others employed in 1304 were Isabelle Cutard, Gunhilde de Bonn, Dyonis and Desiderata de Milleton, Emma de Falling, Matilda Bate (whose father was a furnace man), Joanna Cole and Agnes Sludde. Slag was usually broken by hand (by men) or at the crushers. However, Mattillid de Suthecon was paid '3d for breaking black ore' in July 1304. Not many 'assistants' were named, but they were almost certainly children or young people. One was Richard Le Wowere (or Lehbware), possibly the son of William, another of the furnace men. Agnes Oppenhulle's son, Adam, was also occasionally employed 'working at the water course' or 'lifting earth around the boles'. His wages of 2d for four and a half days suggest that he was a child. As many as nine 'assistants' (probably boys) were also paid for 'blowing the bellows'. These women and children at the Calstock lead smelters were all employed directly by the Mines Royal, and were supervised by an 'overseer'. The washers were paid about 5d per week, and their assistants 3d.

These mines and smelters on the Tamar ceased to operate with the coming of the plague in the mid 14th century. Large-scale lead mining was not undertaken in the area again until the 19th century, when a smelter was built at Weir Quay (Pb2), near Bere Alston. Sisters, sixteen year-old Elizabeth and twelve year-old Ruth Williams, worked there in 1851.

In Cornwall, women and young people were also employed at the lead smelter at Restronguet Point, on the Carrick Roads (Pb3). They included fifteen year-olds Daniel Deeble, Mathew Bray and Edward Lewin (in 1841); sixteen year-olds Nicholas Green, William Nettle and John Roberts (in 1851), plus fifty-six year-old Mary Ann Martin and fourteen year-old Benjamin Pascoe (in 1861). In the same year, fifty-nine year-old widow Ann Bailey was recorded as a 'former worker at the smelter'. It was only latterly accepted that work which took people into contact with lead fumes resulted in serious (and often fatal) damage to health. For those who survived, there were almost certainly long-term effects. This was dangerous work, with probably one of the highest mortality rates across the mining industries.

Copper Smelters

It was eventually found to be more economic to take Cornish copper to a coal source for smelting, rather than shipping the coal to Cornwall, due to the very high fuel requirement. However, there was a brief window when attempts were made at local smelting, when the coal duty was lifted for Cornwall in 1710. Most ventures were short lived, the more successful being at Polruddan, St. Austell (Cu1) and at Copperhouse Creek, Hayle (Cu2), both operating in the mid 18th century. One hundred and fifty were employed at the latter, probably including boys. High mortality rates were recorded, due to arsenic poisoning and heat exhaustion.

Tin Smelters

The earliest records of women and children working at the tin smelters come from the cost books for the Newham and Callenick Smelters near Truro (Sn1). These came into pre-eminence at the very beginning of the 18th century, as new and far more efficient reverbatory furnaces (using coal instead of charcoal) were introduced into Cornwall.

From 1703, women were recorded as the main labour force for barrowing coal, bricks or lime from the shore to the smelter, where they were paid about 2½ d per ton. Among those named were Martha Crips, Elizabeth Traffon, and Ann Stevens.

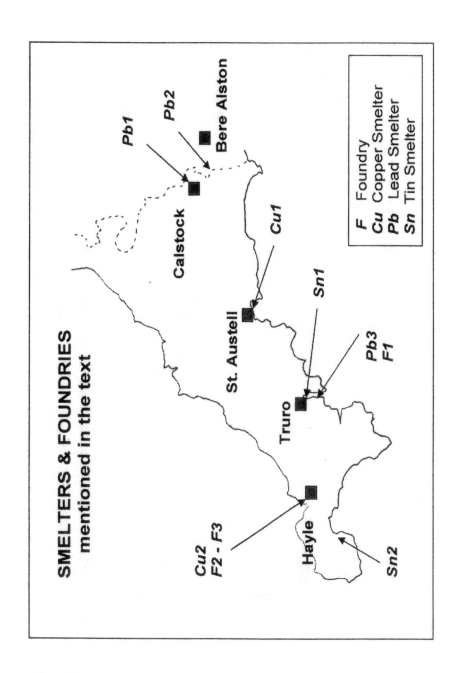

Fig. 14

Others were barrowing and sifting 'culm' (cinders) at the smelter. Among the women paid for this work at Newham were Eddy Caper (or Capow), Addy Chafer, Marjory Hawke, Katherine Rogerman, Joana (or Jenifer) Thomas, Mary Whalley, and Honor and Mary Wolfe (or Woolfe). They were paid about 6d per day. They often worked with an assistant, and were usually paid as a team. In 1704, there is also a reference to 'washing anti' (antinomy), which had probably come from mines in St. Issey or St. Endellion. Both the carrying of coal and the sieving of cinders would have been dusty and dirty work, and these women must have looked more like colliers by the end of their working day!

There are not many other references to women or children working at the tin smelters of Cornwall and Devon. However, forty-four year-old Mary Curnow of Lelant was described as a tin smelter in 1841, as were sisters Amelia and Kate Rowe of Chenhalls, St. Erth in 1891. The latter were possibly employed at the Chyandour Smelter (Sn 2).

Iron Foundry Workers

The largest and most successful foundries in the South West were the Perran Foundry (F1) near Penryn (1791-1879), and Harvey's Foundry (F2) at Hayle (1779-1903). These were major employers in their time, with the Perran works employing 400 workers in its heyday. However, there were other smaller ventures as well, such as the Copperhouse Foundry, Hayle (operated by Sandys) from 1820 to 1867 (F3).

These foundries regularly employed young boys, but records of women or girls are rare. Most of our information comes from the Employment Commission of 1842 or census material. In 1841, one hundred and eighty-two foundry employees at the Harvey's, Perran and Copperhouse Foundries were boys under eighteen years of age, and sixty-three of them were under thirteen years old. The children's working day was usually 6 a.m. to 6 p.m. in summer, and from 7 a.m. to 7 p.m. in winter, with a half hour break for breakfast, and one hour for lunch.

In the pattern shop, the youngest boys made simple moulds, or barrowed fuel. Among them were fifteen-year old Benjamin Bowden of Phillack (in 1841), fourteen-year old William Barden of Hayle (in 1851). In the smith's shop, they attended the bellows and fires, and also helped with some of the hammering. Older boys were taught to turn lathe screws, and then to use the lathes themselves. These 'inside boys' started at 4d per day, increasing to a maximum of 2s. Eventually, they might train to be fitters in the engine shops. There were also labouring boys who worked outside, and were paid 8 or 9d per day. Other young boys working at the Hayle foundries (but whose precise task is unclear) included fifteen year-olds Henry Hendra, Henry Woolcock, Edwin and George Watts, and Samuel Winnen (in 1841), thirteen year-old Richard Penberthy, and fifteen year-olds Robert Northey and John Stickland (in 1851), and twelve-year old Thomas Henry Michell, thirteen year-old Richard Luke, and fourteen year-olds Richard Gilbert, Tobias Michell and William Oliver (in 1861).

The foundries were not a very healthy place to work and, in 1841, the employees are described as 'sallow in appearance'. In that year, two boys had lost an eye 'in play', and a third had lost three fingers in the hammer mill. A fourth boy was lame, but this accident had occurred previously, while he was working at Wheal Vor mine.

Women and girls sometimes seem to be involved in other aspects of the iron foundry industry. Unusually, forty year-old Jane Hodge of West Turnpike, St. Austell was described as an 'iron founder' in 1841. In the same year thirty-five year-old Grace Roberts of Redruth worked as a wire weaver, twenty-one year-old Elizabeth Hosking and seventy year-old Mary Sarah (both of Camborne) were making sieves and pins respectively. Mysteriously, fifteen year-old Elizabeth Vivian (also of Camborne) was described as a 'mechanic', and her father an 'iron founder'. Later, in 1861, twenty-six year-old Mary J. Bishop, of Perran Downs, was described as an iron foundry labourer.

Assaying

One of the on-going and important tasks at the metalliferous mines was to establish the percentage of the metal content in the ore. Since it was the metal content that determined market value, accuracy was crucial for both the managers who were selling the commodity, and for the miners who accepted 'bargains' (working contracts) on the basis of the amount of metal they recovered, not on the amount of ore-bearing rock raised.

At most mines, there would be at least one assayer, working at the assay or sampling office. In the larger mines, the assayer might have an assistant, and it seems that sometimes these assistants were women.

One of the best records we have is of a Miss Bickerleg, who worked for many years with Mr. Charles Davis, the assayer at Dolcoath.

We are told in the Troon Women's Institute interviews that Miss Bickerleg wore a black dress, a wide white apron and the typical 'bal maiden's bonnet'. Around the room were shelves for the tin ore samples, with the smelting furnace at one end. Each sample was laid out on a shelf on thick white paper about one foot square, and meticulously labelled with the miner's name and mine location from which it was taken. Miss Bickerleg worked on the samples on a large central table. Each was carefully brushed into labelled earthenware crucibles. After smelting, Miss Bickerleg would then brush every tiny fragment of separated tin onto small brass scales. To ensure nothing was lost, she used a hare's foot, which she said 'was so fine that no tin could be trapped in the fur'. This sample was then placed in an envelope, sealed, marked with the weight and details and returned to its original paper on the shelf.

Miss Bickerleg was ever conscious of her need to be accurate and often said, 'We must be very careful about this, as it means the men's living.' She had the reputation of 'knowing as much about tin' as the assayer and mine captains (managers) with whom she worked.

Two others who may have worked in the sampling rooms were twenty-three year-old Margaret E. Bennet of Illogan (1881) and twenty-one year-old Emily Richards of Camborne (1891), as both were described as 'sample refiners'.

Elizabeth Ashton, Chemist Extraordinaire

In the latter part of the 19th century, a lone light often burned through the night, out on the cliffs at Hawke's Point, near Carbis Bay. This was not a navigation aid, but Elizabeth Ashton and her husband, Edward, working away at their 'furnace house'. Elizabeth had trained as a chemist alongside her husband (probably in London) in the 1860s. By 1871, they had opened chemist shops in Hayle, St. Just and St. Ives (in partnership with Edward's brother). In 1883, they leased the abandoned Wheal Fanny Adela and re-opened it as Hawke's Point Mine, but it failed as a commercial venture. Subsequently, they worked the mine for cobalt, nickel and copper themselves, presumably preparing chemicals for use in their pharmaceutical and photography business. The ore would be dressed at the nearest convenient point at surface, and then taken to the 'furnace house' for assaying, refining and smelting. Elizabeth was described as being as capable a chemist as her husband.

Around 1905, Elizabeth, tired of the effort of the work, reputedly took matters into her own hands and pulled down some of the props, effectively closing the mine.

Chapter 7

At the Explosives Works

One might be forgiven for thinking that there could not be a much more dangerous place for women and children to work than at the mines and quarries in Cornwall. However, there were places where they were even more at risk: these were the various gunpowder mills and explosives factories.

Gunpowder Mills

Gunpowder was the first explosive used in the mines in Cornwall, and it was commonly in use by 1800. Originally, it came from Somerset, but as it was dangerous to transport, and easily denatured, it was not long before powder mills were being built in Cornwall.

For safety reasons, gunpowder mills were usually situated deep in woodland, where it was cool, and with a suitable water supply to provide power. In the early days, part of the woodland would be coppiced to provide charcoal (one of the ingredients). The mill buildings were built of wood, and often divided from each other by stone walls or banks and ditches for protection. Obviously, the slightest spark or fire could have terrible consequences, so employees had to be extra vigilant, and many protective methods were put in place.

Paths and doorways between the buildings were covered with damp hemp matting, and had foot baths, to reduce the risk of fire. Workers had to avoid dust and grit getting into contact with gunpowder. All utensils used were either copper or wood. Floors were covered with tanned hides, and employees had to wear slippers. All containers were covered with leather.

The first gunpowder mill to be built in Cornwall was by Nichols and Gill in Cosawes Wood, near Ponsanooth in 1809 (Fig 15) (G1). Another was built nearby in the woods at Kennal Vale in 1811 (G2). Cosawes Mill was incorporated into Kennal Vale sometime before 1844. By the 1860s, the largest mills were at Kennal Vale; and also at Trago Mills (G4) and Herodsfoot (G5) which constituted the East Cornwall Gunpowder Co. A smaller mill was also operating at Bishop's Wood in St. Allen (G3) from about 1864 until 1879. In Devon, gunpowder was also produced by the Dartmoor Company in Tavistock, and at Cherry Brook near Postbridge. It seems that women and children were employed on a regular basis at these works (certainly in Cornwall) but just how many is unclear.

Gunpowder was made from imported saltpetre, and sulphur. High grade charcoal, the third ingredient, was usually made in special sealed iron retorts on site. The first step was to carefully sieve out any gravel from the three ingredients, and then pulverise them under stone-edged wheels.

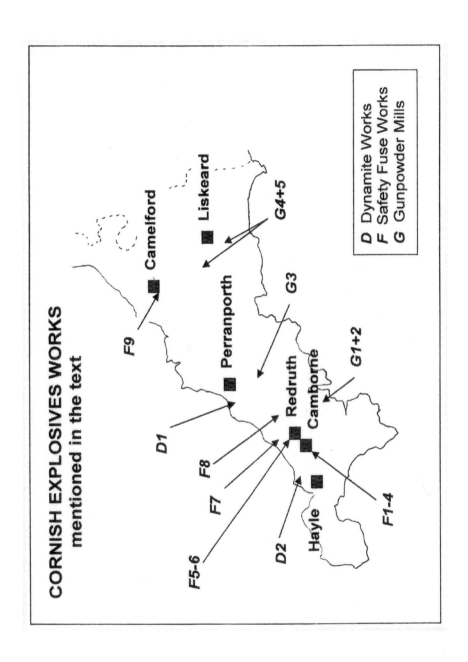

Fig. 15

The ingredients were then mixed in the incorporating mills, moistened and made into 'mill-cake'. After this, it was pressed into sheets, re-granulated, dusted and carefully dried.

The first serious explosion in Cornwall happened very shortly after Cosawes Mill was opened, in February 1809:

'One of the carpenters was directed to make a small alteration in the machine that works the sieves, and the man who had care of the house was preparing to remove all the powder but was prevailed on to let it remain, upon an assurance that only a wooden mallet would be used. Soon after, the neighbourhood was alarmed by an explosion, and the manager of the works found the carpenter and the other workman, with two women, blown about twenty yards from the ruin, and dreadfully wounded. The men and one woman, survived only a few hours; the other woman anguished until next morning. Another man and a girl, who were working in an adjoining house, escaped unhurt.' (RCG 5th Aug 1809)

In February 1826, an elderly woman was killed in an explosion at Kennal Vale:

'We regret to state that an accident which has been attended with melancholy results, occurred at the powder mills near Ponsanooth on Friday last. About half-past twelve o'clock, an explosion took place in the mixing house in which four persons – three men and an old woman – at their usual employment. Two of the men escaped with comparatively little injury, but the woman, whose name is Elizabeth Ritter, was so dreadfully scorched that she died on Friday night; the

third man whose name was Weeks, survived until Sunday morning, without suffering much pain, when he also expired. Although it is generally difficult to account for accidents which occur at powder mills, in the present instant it has been ascertained that the fatal event was occasioned by the negligence of the old woman, who fell victim to her own want of caution. She had been roasting potatoes in a house at a considerable distance from the works, and had unconsciously carried a small spark of fire on her clothes from thence to the mill. This was seen almost immediately on her entrance, but before it could be prevented, it fell, and the explosion instantly followed.' (WB 24 Feb 1826)

Only five months later, in June 1826, a man and boy were killed in another explosion while sweeping in one of the mills. At Bishop's Wood Mills, in 1864, a number of the girls were packing cartridges and working late into the night. They were allowed to sleep in the granulating room rather than walk home through the woods in the dark. As they were getting up the following morning, there was a large explosion. One of the girls was killed instantly, and another died some hours later. They were Ellen Reynolds and Elizabeth Grose. The watchman's boy was witness to the accident.

Safety Fuse Factories

From 1805, William Bickford, a leather merchant of Tuckingmill, began to produce miner's fuses commercially. Previously, miners had made their own primitive fuses from powder and goose quills, often with fatal results. Bickford's first attempts (a small bag with a narrow tubular fuse made of parchment) also proved to be unpredictable. However, by 1831, he and a local miner, Thomas Davey, had developed a textile fibre fuse with a core of powder that burned reliably. He also patented a machine that could pour gunpowder into fibres at a regular rate, as they were twisted in a rope walk.

Bickford's factory was at Tuckingmill (F3), on the old road between Redruth and Camborne. In 1841, seven girls were employed there (one of whom was under thirteen years-old) along with two boys (also under thirteen). One of the mine surgeons had this to say about the girls:

'There is a manufactory of safety fuse near Camborne at which young females are employed. He finds their health by no means as good as that of the girls at the mine.'

Once Bickford's patent had expired, the Camborne area became the heartland for safety fuse production. Alfred Lanyon opened the British and Foreign Safety Fuse Co. in 1848 at Plain-an-Gwary, Redruth. By 1856, William Brunton (F2) had opened a factory in Pool, which in 1865 employed two men, thirteen females, and one boy. The 1861 census recorded sixty women and girls employed in total at the safety fuse factories in the Redruth, Illogan and Camborne area. Seventeen of these were employed by Thomas Davey (F4) in his own 'powder rope' factory in Camborne. He later opened a fuse factory in Nancekuke, Illogan (F7). Presumably, twenty-three year-old Elizabeth Pope of Illogan Downs, who was described as a 'powder maker' in the 1861 census, was working there.

Fig. 16 Tuckingmill Fuse Factory 1949
Women working at the fuse spinning machines (Courtesy of ICI)

Fig. 17 Tuckingmill Fuse Factory 1949
Women working in the varnishing room (Courtesy of ICI)

One of Bickford's later competitors was William Bennetts, who built a factory in Scorrier, Gwennap in 1865, which he then moved to Roskear in 1871 (Fig. 15) (F1), and to St. Day (F8) in 1875. Edward Tangye (F5) also opened a factory in Redruth.

In the 1881 census, over a hundred females are recorded as working at fuse works in the Camborne-Redruth area. In 1891, the number was slightly lower, at seventy-five. In contrast, there were over two hundred recorded in the 1901 census. (This is in keeping with an estimate, for the year before, of a total employment of five hundred at Bickford's, three hundred at Bennetts' and one hundred at the other safety fuse factories).

Some women were employed in the jute carding and spinning rooms at these factories. Their task was to ensure that the jute (the fibre used for the body of the fuse) was free from any dust or dirt which might cause either uneven burning of the rope, or a spark. Some women filled the hoppers over the funnels which fed the explosive into the spinning machine. Others spun the fuse, operating a machine to ensure the continuous flow of gunpowder (Fig. 16). Women were also employed in the checking, varnishing and measuring rooms (Fig. 17). In 1887, the girls at Tucking Mill were paid just four and a half pence per day, which seems to be a much lower wage than they would receive at the mines. Women continued to be employed at the factory in Tucking Mill until it closed in the 1950s.

Similar safety precautions had to be taken in the fuse factories as at the gunpowder mills, even though smaller quantities of gunpowder were being handled. Messrs Brunton & Co. at Penhallick were the first fuse factory to have a serious accident. This was in April 1861:

'It seems that a few minutes after the girls had resumed work from their dinner half-hour, the powder ... exploded with tremendous force, blew off the roof ... and nearly demolished the walls. It also set the buildings on fire. ... Two girls who had charge of the powder-room, named Blight and Handcock, are dead – both frightfully burned. A boy called Sleeman was found nearly dead, and expired a few minutes afterwards. About 16 other persons, principally girls, are more or less injured, two of them dangerously so'. (West Briton 12th April 1861)

The women who died were Elizabeth Blight (about twenty nine years old), Ann Hancock (thirty years old), both spinning fuses in the fuse room. The third fatality was the engine boy William Sleeman (just fourteen years old) who was in the winding room, adjacent to these women, at the time of the accident. Three women jumped to safety from the winding room, one of whom suffered a head injury and subsequent convulsions. Two other women were severely burnt, and third had been hit on the head by debris. The cause of the explosion was uncertain; although failure of one of the pieces of machinery in the fuse room was suggested. Verdicts of accidental death were passed at the inquest.

Four years later, on 27th April 1865, there was another explosion at Brunton's. It seems that lessons had not been learnt about the dangers of the most risky operations being carried out upstairs. Again, all except two women escaped;

Elizabeth Vivian (twenty-nine years old) and Ellen Oppy (twenty years old) were trapped and died in the resulting fire. They had also been working upstairs in the fuse spinning room. Two other women in the adjacent winding room were slightly burnt.

More advanced fuses using guncotton were produced at Thomas Davey's Nancekuke Fuse Works, and at a similar factory that was opened in Camelford (F9) by Kellow and Short (the latter to supply the Delabole Slate Quarries). Similarly, the women and girls at these factories had to carefully clean the cotton to remove any foreign bodies that may cause a spark. They also worked in the drying and sifting houses. On 9th September 1862, not long after the opening of the Nancekuke Fuse Works, four women were killed instantly in an explosion. Two more died shortly afterwards from their injuries, and three were severely burnt. Some of the men and boys working there were also badly injured. Those who died were fifty year-old widow Betsy Haughton, thirty-one and twenty-eight year-old sisters Mary and Harriet Johns, twenty year-old Nanny Andrews and sixteen year-olds Harriet Reynolds and Elizabeth Thomas. It is thought the explosion was caused by freak lightning striking through the window. Thomas Davey remarked at the inquest *'I do not think that any of the unfortunate victims caused the explosion ... all of them were remarkably well behaved and steady'*.

Ten years later, in 1872, there was an explosion at Bickford's Fuse factory. Seven girls were killed: Mary Ellen and Louisa Sims of Beacon, Elizabeth Carah, Annie James and Martha Towan of Camborne (all reelers), also Emily Climo of

Camborne and Ellen Goldsworthy of Beacon Hill (who were spinners). Fanny Bennetts was seriously burned and six others less seriously injured. Sarah Ann Cock, one of the survivors, was witness at the inquest.

In February 1875, there was an explosion and subsequent fire at the St. Day Fuse Factory:

'The number of deaths from the explosion at the St. Day Fuse Works is now five, the fifth being the girl Margaretta Long, aged 18, who escaped death by burning by jumping out of window, but who died from the injuries received and shock to the nervous system at midnight on Sunday. Those dead are Ann Davey (37), Elizabeth Jane James (29), Christina Mitchell (17), Elizabeth Ann Pooley (14), Margaretta Long (18). Inasmuch as only the remains of Long could be identified, the inquest was held on her body, and in it was included the inquest on the bodies of the four other persons not identified. The remains of these four appeared to be nothing more than pieces of charred wood; these however, were placed in oak coffins, which had been made by order of Sir F. M. Williams Bart., MP., the owner of the factory. (A foreman and seven other women or girls worked there. The others were injured but survived') WB 25.2.1875

Again, all had been trapped in the upper story of the factory. At last, new legislation was enacted to make it illegal to prepare explosives in two-storey buildings. Thomas Davey then moved the factory to a new building in Little Beside.

High Explosives Factories

By the 1880s, dynamite was found to be a more effective explosive for mining operations, and the days of the gunpowder mills drew to a close.

New dynamite factories were opened in Hayle (in 1881), and out on Cligga Head in Perranzabuloe (in 1891). They were the National Explosives Factory and the British and Colonial Explosives Company, respectively. Women and children were still employed in these operations.

The women and girls worked in small units in isolated huts on the cliffs or in the dunes (Fig. 18). At Cligga Head they worked in groups of three. They had to wear carpet slippers or rubber boots, and were searched every morning by a matron or forewoman for anything that could inadvertently cause a spark. At both factories, the workers in the 'danger areas' wore red clothes; the women with red cloaks or wrappers (Fig. 19). The girls worked at hand operated machines producing tubes of dynamite or gelignite, which they then wrapped and packed carefully in boxes. Fig. 18 shows two boys holding the boxes in which they presumably carried the cartridges away for safe storage.

The 1891 census records about 20 females employed at the dynamite works, and living in the Hayle area, with none recorded for the St. Agnes area (which was when the 'British and Colonial' was only just opening). However, by 1892, thirty girls were employed there, with vacancies for another thirty.

Fig. 18 National Explosives Co., early 1890s
Employees outside a Dynamite mixing house (Courtesy of Bryan Earl)

Fig. 19 National Explosives Co. employees, early 1890s,
Including 'cartridging girls' (Courtesy of Bryan Earl)

It was observed that girls working at the Hayle factory often suffered from headaches, and that they had a yellow colouration to their skin and hair, probably due to exposure to phenols. At Hayle, on 19th October 1899, one engine boy (William Harvey) was killed and one man injured in an explosion. Two women also died in an explosion at the cordite press during WWI.

The numbers employed at both sites increased considerably during the Boer War and WWI, with the increased demand for armaments. After the Explosives Act of 1911, women were trained at Camborne School of Mines to work in the quality control laboratories. A Miss Morley and Miss Crowle were photographed working at the Hayle laboratories in 1917. By 1919, however, with the war over and mining in Cornwall almost at an end, there was little continuing demand for explosives. Both dynamite factories had closed by 1920.

A Dangerous Place to Work

The total number of casualties at these gunpowder, fuse and explosives works (forty-nine deaths reported for Cornwall over a hundred year period) was very low compared to the number of fatalities at the mines. However, what is startling is the proportion of these who were women or children: twenty nine females and three boys (71% of the deaths for which the gender is given). This is almost certainly because they constituted the major part of the workforce. For instance, of sixteen employees at Brunton's Fuse Factory in 1865, there were thirteen women and girls, and one boy.

This high ratio can also be seen in the photograph of the employees of the National Explosives Co. (Fig. 19). The women and girls were also at higher risk, as only a proportion of the male employees worked in close proximity to the explosives, whereas the women and girls were handling them on a daily basis.

These women and children not only needed a fine dexterous skill to handle such dangerous substances, but also had huge responsibilities laid on their shoulders. The smallest 'foreign body' in the fibres or explosives, or the generation of the tiniest spark could spell disaster. Their own lives, and the lives of others, depended on their continuous care, concentration and attention to detail.

Chapter 8

Women Traders and Managers

While women and girls were commonly employed in the mines and clay works of the South West, as labourers or servants, it comes as a quite a surprise to discover a handful of women who became mine managers, clay merchants or tin traders in their own right. Some made a considerable contribution to the success of the industries in which they were involved.

The earliest record is of a group of women who were involved in the Medieval and Tudor tin trade in Devon. Most seem to have taken over the tin trading role on the death of their husbands. 'Isobell of Northworthi' and 'Sarra of Holne' took tin to Ashburton, and Clarice Lyne took tin to Chagford, for coinage in 1303. Later, in 1477, Agnes Stannon took Henry Wynneslond to the Stannary Court at Tavistock for selling her corrupt tin at Buchland Monachorum, two years previously. In 1531, Rachel Bownde and Matilda Browne took tin to Plympton, Elizabeth and (or) Isabella Bradeley, Alice Nosworthy, Joanna Wyncheat, Elizabeth Dolberre and Catherine Hamlyn all sold tin at Ashburton, and Alice Hanworthy (Hanfforde) took tin to Tavistock. Later in the same century, Joan Winsland was leasing a tin mill at

Walkhampton, and Juliana Rede leased a knocking and blowing mill at Keigella Borowe.

Another group of women tin traders, who must have known each other well, were all operating in Truro in the early 18th century. From the cost books, we find that Charity Casier, Barbara Collins, Mrs Jael Foote, Mary Ley, Elizabeth Smith, as well as Mary and Ursula Thomas, brought tin to be smelted at Newham in 1709. Most of these women were probably widows and would have inherited their business on the death of their husbands. We know very little of them, except that Charity continued trading over many years, and had a mixed reputation which involved her in several court appearances. When Charity died in 1725, Grace Hoblyn seems to have taken over her tin trading business.

A further group of women 'in management' were working during the mid 19th century. The only known female manager of a tin mine for this period was Lydia Taylor, who is recorded at Wheal Lovell in Wendron between 1840 and 1845. It seems that Lydia probably became mine manager after estrangement from her second husband, and when her son left for Canada. Under her management, there were several disputes over mine boundaries and payments, and also two fatal accidents. Thomas Dunstan died from a fall in July 1840, and William Oliver in February 1841.

It seems that Lydia was also involved in South Wheal Towan (also, unsurprisingly, known as Wheal Lydia). Her son had appointed another manager there in his absence, but Lydia was sometimes called upon to intervene. Lydia lived at the counthouse at Wheal Lovell, and despite neither mine seeming to make a huge fortune, could afford a French governess for her daughter Charlotte. There is no further record of Lydia or Charlotte, after Wheal Lovell was bought out in 1845. It may be that they followed Lydia's son to Canada.

There was at least one woman trader who made a less than positive name for herself. She was a Mrs. Gully. A complaint was brought against her in 1841 by the Rev. Linell Buler (sic), for selling shares in Wheal Trevenson, a non-existent mine. This earned her the ill reputation of 'Bal-seller'.

The main body of 19th century women managers and traders, though, was at the east end of the county, in St. Austell. They were all involved in the china clay trade.

Sarah Michell managed Carbean, Bluebarrow (Bunny), and Yondertown Clay Works from 1848 until about 1868, after the death of her husband. In 1851, she sent samples of her clay to the Great Exhibition at Crystal Palace. These appear in the catalogue described as:

Michell, Sarah, St. Austell - Producer *'White china-clay, for manufacturing china and earthenware, also for bleaching paper, calico etc.'.*

Phillipa Lovering also took over management of her husband's business interests at Lower Ninestones, when he died, in 1834. Phillipa was in her late forties, and continued to manage these works until her son, John Lovering Jnr., was of age (by about 1845). The Lower Ninestone Cost Books 1828-1836 were written by Phillipa, so it seems that she was working as her husband's bookkeeper for many years before his death (Fig. 20). Phillipa and her son subsequently took leases on Stents in 1850, West Goonbarrow in 1868, and Carbean and Bluebarrow in 1870. It seems that Phillipa was a very able woman, described as *'a lady of great strength of character and activity'* and *'a capable business woman.'*

A Mrs. Thriscot (Truscott) managed Caudledown after the death of her husband Thomas, from about 1858 and Mrs. Margaret Spargo was described as a China Clay Merchant in Gunnislake in 1893. Very little is known about these two women.

However, the most notable female 'clay baron' must have been Rebecca Martin who managed several large clay works and was largely responsible for initiating more successful co-operative practices in the clay industry in the mid 19th century. She was born in St. Austell in 1799 and married John Martin, who was heavily involved in the development of the major clay works in the St. Austell area from about 1835. They lived in Blowing House, St. Austell and, when John died in 1844, Rebecca took over the responsibility for the running of their various businesses. It seems that she inherited considerable holdings in the Cornwall China Stone and Clay Co., which failed in 1848, but, at the same time, she was one of the five independent producers who controlled over one third of the china clay output in Cornwall.

In 1849, she seemed to be the prime mover in pushing for an agreement between producers to regulate china clay prices,

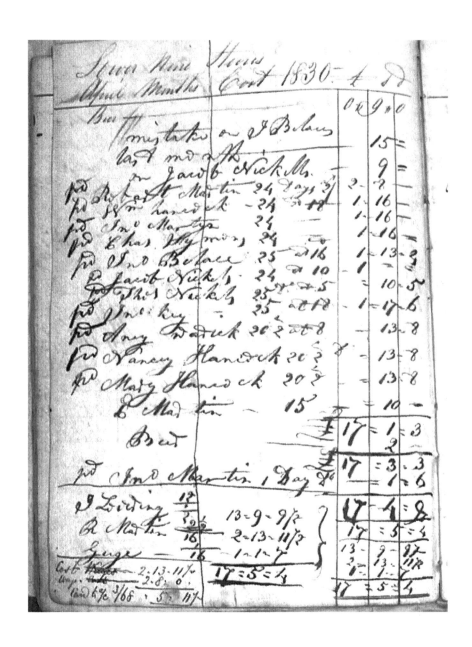

Fig. 20 Lower Ninestones Cost Book April 1830
These accounts were entered by Philippa Lovering

Courtesy of China Clay Country Park Mining & Heritage Centre

and to put an end to the practice of allowing purchasers to accumulate enormous debts. Steam engines were introduced relatively late into the clay works, from 1837, so, since Rebecca was selling an old steam engine at Little Treviscoe in 1851, her works had presumably been among the first to install this technology. By 1852, Rebecca appears to have been in partnership with Phillipa and John Lovering with a view to exploiting Carnclaze Tin Mine for china clay.

In 1858, she was managing at least six works: Carvear, Screeda, Lansalson, Huel Virgin, Mellangoose, Little Treviscoe, and possibly North Goonbarrow as well. The clay produced from these works in that year totalled 6,900 tons. In 1862, she also took over the lease for Lee Moor Clay, Brick and Tile Works. Interestingly, in the 1861 census, Rebecca is recorded as being blind, so presumably these later transactions must have been carried out despite considerable disability. Although she had three sons, William Langdon, Thomas and Edward, all of whom were involved in the clay business, it seems that during her lifetime she held the control of the family ventures. She died in 1863, at the age of 64.

Rebecca was described in this way:

'She was a lady of great determination and, in spite of her small size, was more than a match for her sons or any other clay producers. Her reputation for forthrightness did not enhance her popularity amongst her rivals, but they respected her nevertheless because she was honest and fair in her dealings with them.'

The death of these formidable women 'clay barons' seems to herald an end of an era of women managers and traders. It is possible that women may have been managing mines or other enterprises during WWI while men were engaged in war service. In the early 20th century it is believed that a 'Miss Lidgey' (of Rough Street, Lanner) managed Magdalen Mine, Ponsanooth. As there was a Lidgey family involved in managing the Gunpowder Works, nearby at Kennal Vale, this mysterious Miss Lidgey may have belonged to that dynasty. No other records of women mine managers during WWI have yet come to light. Miss Lidgey appears to have been the last in a line of some very exceptional women.

Appendix 1

Summaries of Interviews with "Bal Maidens", conducted in 1841, for the 1842 Royal Commission Report on Employment of Women and Children at the Mines

(NB The numbers relate to the interviews in the appendix of the report.)

No. 6 Grace Bowden (17 years): Trethellan

Grace began work at the mine at 16. For 2 years previously, she had made straw bonnets, but had to leave due to poor health. She was in good health when interviewed. Her tasks were spalling or cobbing, but she had no preference for either. She earned 9d per day. She lodged 2 miles from the mine, and brought a pasty for lunch. She was attending Sunday School.

No. 7 Martha Williams (11 years): Trethellan

Martha had been picking for 1 year. She lived with her widowed mother in Redruth, 5 miles from the mine; her father having died 2 years previously. She usually had bread and milk for breakfast, pasty with meat in it for lunch, and potato with tea for supper. She would go to bed about 7 pm. She had been to day school before starting at the mine. She was described as healthy.

No. 18 Mary Ann Roscorle (12 years): Tresavean

Mary was at the picking tables. She had been raised in the workhouse, and was now in lodgings. She left there at 6 am, and stopped work at 5.30 pm.

No. 19 Jane Uren (16 years): Tresavean

Jane had been at the mine for 6 years. She had recently been moved to the cobbing floor, where she would dress 1.5 barrows (2.25 cwt) per day. She lived 1.5 miles from the mine. 5 of her 9 siblings also worked there.

No. 20 Mary Johns (14 years): Tresavean

Mary had previously been in service and thought that her health was better in the last year she had been at the mine. She was employed at spalling or barrowing. She found the work heavy, and suffered pains in her back and side, especially when doing the latter. She worked in all weathers, sometimes getting very wet; but rarely caught cold. She had previously attended a day school, and had been going to Sunday School since working at the mine.

No. 21 Elizabeth Larkeek (18 years): Tresavean

Elizabeth had been a bucker at Tresavean for 5 months, but working at other mines for 2 years previously. Her pay had recently been reduced from 6 to 8 barrows for 1s. She had pains in her left arm, depending on the weather. She had been to day school, and was now attending Sunday School.

No. 28 Eliza Allen (20 year): Consols

Eliza had worked at the mine for 2 years, firstly 'with her father' and then cobbing. She suffered from shortness of breath, and could not stand for long. She was only earning half of her wage of 18s per month. Her feet were often wet, causing her to catch cold. She had never been to school but could sew a little. The surgeon commented on her delicate constitution and 'disorder of the system'.

No. 32 Anna Wasley (20 years): Ale & Cakes Mine

Anna had worked here for 7 years, and had been suffering from shortness of breath for 12 months. She worked 10 hours per day, from 7 am to 5.30 pm with 30 minutes for dinner. Her 6 siblings were also working at the mines.

No. 33 Sally Fall (19 years): Gwennap Mines

Sally had been working at various mines for 8 years, and was now bucking. She had strained herself while lifting a heavy weight the previous year, and was still suffering shortness of breath. Her 5 siblings all went to the mines at an early age, after their father had died. She had never been to school. (NB. The 1841 census shows a Sarah Faul, of the same age, in Truro Infirmary 2 months later.)

No. 45 Eliza Evans (17 years): Budnick Consols?

Eliza had tried to work at the mines, generally picking, but suffered severe headaches. An older sister was working at the frames at Budnick Consols, and a brother of 15 worked underground.

No. 46 Fanny Francis (17 years): United Mines

Fanny had been a bal maiden for 6 years. She had been having fits for 3 months, after a fall while barrowing. She also suffered from dyspepsia and skin complaints. Her mother was widowed, and 4 siblings were also at the mine. Fanny had previously attended day school, and was now a Sunday School teacher.

No. 47 Jane Sandoe (17 year): Wheal Gorland

Jane was cobbing, and had not been strong enough for bucking. She lived 3 miles from the mine. She suffered from 'gastrodynia'. The oldest of her 9 siblings had all started work at the mine at about 10 years. They all attended Sunday School.

No. 60 Christina Morcom (53 years): Gwennap Mines

Christina had worked here from the age of 10 years. About 20 years previously she had begun to suffer from lumbago, which she attributed to her mine work,

No. 61 Jane Jewell (21 years): Consols

Jane felt ill at the mine and thought this was due to the warm mundic waters. She had only been working for 2 weeks, but was unable to continue. Her 50 year-old father had also been employed there, but was in decline.

No. 86 Martha Buckingham (14 years): Consolidated Mines

Martha had been working here for 4 years, mostly at the picking table, but occasionally she was called on to barrow, riddle, or spall. She found barrowing the hardest, especially if it was all day, as it gave her back pain. Picking was normally done under a shed with no sides, so that her feet were often cold and wet. As she had no dry shoes to change into, she sometimes caught cold.

Martha lived at Bissoe Bridge, 3 miles from the mine. Her waking day was 18 hours, and her working day normally 10 hours. However, for a week or fortnight in every month (at sampling) this would be 14 hours, when she became very tired. When sampling was over she was allowed 1 day off, but she was not paid overtime for this extra work. Martha said that work was available continuously during the winter but, due to water shortages, this was not always so in the summer.

She took a pasty or hoggan for dinner, which could be warmed in the dry at the mine. The girls ate together in the dinner shed, and were allowed 1 hour. They did not have a mid-morning break, so by 9 or 10 am they were usually hungry, and would eat some of their pasty while still working, when the surface captain wasn't looking.

When interviewed, Martha described having 'overheated her blood' from carrying too much and that she was continuing to 'break out'. The mine surgeon reported that she was generally healthy despite a 'cough and papulous eruption'.

Martha was one of 7 children, and her mother widowed. Years earlier, her father had gone to Scotland and had been sending money for the family, however, he had died when Martha was 6. Her older siblings went to work at the mine to support the family, but she had 1 younger sibling at home. One of her brothers, who worked at Poldice Mine, was chronically ill. She was attending Sunday School. (NB. From the 1841 census her mother appears to be Delia Buckingham of Bissoe, although Martha and her 30 year-old sister Mary were not described as working at the mine.)

No. 87 Mary Verran (14 years): Consolidated Mines

Mary had first been employed at picking at 10 years old. She was now barrowing. This gave her pains in the back, which continued at night. Other girls complained of similar problems.

Three or four girls, who were spalling or riddling, had been taken home as they felt faint or sick. Mary lived 1 mile from the mine and would get up at 4.30 or 5 am. Christmas Day and Good Friday were holidays, a half day was allowed for Whitsuntide, and 2 hours off at Midsummer and Christmas Eve. Most of the girls took plum and potato hoggans for lunch, finding the half hour break was too short. At home she would have fish and potatoes, stew or roast potatoes for supper. She had attended day school before working at the mine, and now went to Sunday School twice on a Sunday.

No. 88 Elizabeth Curnow (24 years): Consolidated Mines

Elizabeth had been working at the mine since she was 16. Her usual work was cobbing, and she was paid per barrow dressed. At sampling (for 1-2 weeks per month) she worked from 7 am until 8 pm. Her legs and feet became very cold in winter, as the cobbing house ran with water and damp ore fell about her feet. She lived 2 miles from the mine, and took a pasty for lunch, which could be warmed at the mine. She found half an hour not long enough for croust time. Due to lack of strength and appetite she had only worked for 2 days in the last 2 months. She sometimes took work in service when she felt stronger. She found mine work harder than in service, but liked being able to finish earlier.

No. 89 Christina Pascoe (17 years): Consolidated Mines

Christina had been picking for 2 years, from the age of 12. She then went to the spalling floors or was barrowing. With these outside tasks she had become breathless and had fallen into decline. She had been moved into the cobbing house 7 months previously, which she found easier. However, her feet were often wet, and she was still experiencing breathlessness and pains in her back. She was cobbing 6 barrows per day for 8d. She sometimes dressed another 1 or 2 barrows overtime. She lived 1 mile from the mine and would get up at 6 am. To support her widowed mother she had household jobs at home, and would go to bed between 10 and 11 pm. Her father had been injured at Wood Mine, had fallen into consumption, and had died 8 months before.

No. 103 Elizabeth Hocking (16 years): Charlestown Mines

Elizabeth began at the racking frames at the age of 13, but for 3 years she had been spalling. She found the work very hard, causing chronic pain in her limbs, and sometimes her back. This pain did not always go away on lying down. About once a month she worked overtime. Her waking day was from 5.30 am to 9 or 10 pm. She gave her wages to her mother. (NB. The 1851 census shows her living on Tywardreath Highway, and still working at the mine).

No. 104 Elizabeth Davey (17 years): Charlestown Mines

Elizabeth had been in service before starting at the mines. Since then she had worked for 18 months at the racking frames. She admitted that she was liable to 'take cold'. The mine surgeon described her as 'having a good colour but rather delicate'. (NB. She is probably the Elizabeth Davy of the East Turnpike Road, noted in the 1841 Census)

No. 112 Mary Buller (15 years): Fowey Consols

Mary's work was cobbing and spalling copper ore, and she had been at the mine for 6 years. She was usually paid at a daily rate, but one day a week she would be paid by 'the task'. On these occasions, once she had dressed her allocated amount, she could go home, otherwise she finished at 5 pm. She had previously attended day school for 3 years, but had forgotten what she had learnt.

No. 113 Caroline Coom (11 years): Fowey Consols

Caroline had been picking for 2 years. Despite describing her work as pleasant and not tiring, she sometimes became very cold, and had suffered a fever from the time she started work. She was paid by the day, and usually finished at 5 pm. She was currently attending a Sunday School.

Appendix 2

Summaries of Interviews with Boys at the Mines of Devon & Cornwall conducted in 1841, for the 1842 Royal Commission Report on Employment of Women and Children at the Mines

(NB The numbers relate to the interviews in the appendix of the report.)

No. 2 John Henry Martin (12 years): Trethellan

John went to work underground at Wheal Brewer at 11, despite being lame from a hip infection, where he worked the 'blowing machine' at 120 fathoms. He could climb 'tolerably well'. Currently he was at surface, washing ore. Despite his feet being wet all day he did not catch cold. He claimed the work did not tire him. He lived 30 minutes walk from the mine and started work at 7 am, with a pasty for dinner at 12 noon. Holidays were Christmas Day and Good Friday. His wages were normally 12s (with 2d deducted for the doctor), which he gave to his mother. He only earned 10s the previous month due to snow on the picking tables. He changed clothes at home, if wet. He had tea with bread and treacle for breakfast, and potatoes for supper. He would go to bed at 7 pm. He had 11 siblings, and his mother kept a small farm. The older children were at the mine; the younger helped around the farm. John had been attending Sunday School.

No. 3 Samuel Tippet (10 years): Trethellan

Samuel had worked 'at the slimes' where he was paid 7s per month. He was now 'washing up' for 10s per month. He lived with his grandfather half a mile from the mine. Sometimes his back and legs were tired. He had milk, water, bread, barley or wheat for breakfast, potato hoggan for dinner, and potatoes (sometimes with pork) for supper. He would go to bed at 8 pm. He had been attending Sunday School for 2 years.

No. 4 William Harris (15 years): Trethellan

William first worked at Tresavean at about 10, but had been at Trethellan for 10 months, riddling or wheeling ore stuff. He would feel tired at the end of the day, He had once poisoned his finger with the 'mundic water'. He earnt 15s per month, giving this to his mother. His mother had been widowed 12 years ago, and he had 4 siblings. His mother had since married a farmhand, and William sometimes helped him on returning from the mine.

No. 5 Thomas Knuckey Martin (14 years): Trethellan

Thomas had worked here for 3 years, and at Tresavean for 2 years previously. He was jigging, and his feet were often wet, with his shoes not always dry the next day. He lived with his grandmother, and had barley bread and butter for breakfast, a potato hoggan at dinner, and potatoes with fish for supper. He had attended day school, and Sunday School since starting at the mines.

No. 9 Henry Francis (16 years): Tresavean

Henry had been underground for 3 years, and was 'turning' or 'beating the borer' at the 75 fathom level. After work he sometimes helped his father on the smallholding. (The surgeon described him as delicate and small for his age.)

No. 10 Thomas Dunstan (16 years): (Tresavean)

Thomas had been underground for 6 months, wheeling ore-stuff, and had been at the mine for 3 years. He worked at 136 fathoms, and sometimes became out of breath on the ladders. He would take food underground, but would not be given any water. He sometimes worked for this father at home.

No. 13 James Stevens (15 years): (Tresavean)

James had worked underground for 7 years (2 years at Wheal Harmony) and was wheeling ore at 146 fathoms. He worked 4 or 5 days a week (but never at night). He would get up at 4 am, and sometimes took his bread and butter breakfast to eat on the way. He ate no food while at work, and had dinner at home. He had 8 siblings, 4 of whom were working. He sometimes attended Sunday School.

No. 22 Richard Uren (11 years): (Tresavean)

Richard had been 'washing up' at Tresavean for 2 years. He lived near the mine. His father had died of consumption 3 years previously.

No. 23 Joseph Odgers Vincent (14 years): (Tresavean)

Joseph was jigging, and had spent 2 of the previous 3 years at Tresavean. Along with other boys, he complained of pain in the loins after 9 hours of work. His feet were generally wet, but he didn't catch cold. Some days he went home at 2 pm., having finished his task. He would soon be moved to riddling. He had 4 years at day school before going to the mine, and had attended Sunday School since.

No. 52 Thomas Fidock (13 years): East Wheal Crofty

Thomas was first employed at Stray Park at 9, where he was buddling. He worked from 7 am to 5 pm, and had 'task' work about once a month. He had attended day school before going to the mines, and Sunday School since.

No. 53 John Richards (13 years): East Wheal Crofty

John had been at the mine for 3 years, and was currently buddling. He would get up at 5.30 am. He had 'task' work once a fortnight, when he left at 2 pm.

No. 57 Michael Allen Nicholls (11 years): United Mines

Michael had been 'engine boy' for 8 months. Once he had received a blow from the handle of the engine, while cleaning.

No. 58 William Bennett: Wheal Kitty

William had worked at surface at Polgooth from 9, and underground (wheeling ore stuff) from 11. He had also worked 6 months underground (at Wheal Kitty) but had been bringing up blood. Currently, he was stamp watching from 5 pm. to 7 am., for 2 weeks out of 3. Every 3 or 6 hours he was taking turns to sleep, by the boilers or some other dry place. He had begun spitting blood again.

No. 63 Charles Manuel (16 years): Carnon

Charles had worked for 2 years at surface and then 3 years below ground (wheeling). After working in poor air, he had been suffering chest pains and spitting black stuff, so that he had been on and off work. Once he had also been injured on the arm by falling rock. He had only worked overtime 3 times when underground, but he spoke of a boy who had worked 5 double shifts in 6 days, the previous week. He was now working at surface and had hardly been off sick. He gave his wages to his father. He had been attending evening school from 6.30 to 8.30 pm., paying 3d per week.

No. 71 Jacob Turner (17 years): Carn Brea Mines

Jacob had worked at surface for many years, but had gone underground 9 months previously. After 5 months he had moved from the 70 and 80 fathom levels to 50 fathoms. Here the air was cold and foul, and he had developed a cough and nose bleed. When climbing the ladders he said 'my heart seems as if it would jump out of my body'. His father, 23 and 24 year-old brothers, and a 29 year-old sister, had all died of consumption. His surviving twin siblings also worked at the mine. The mother believed that 'Poor air ... had done for both of the young men and their father'. The surgeon described Jacob as 'phthiscal'.

No. 79 Richard Bishop (16 years): East Wheal Rose

Richard first worked at surface at 7, and had been employed at Goonavern and Wheal Elizabeth lead mines. He first went underground at 14. He was currently wheeling ore for 6 hour shifts, on a weekly rota. Where he worked the air was quite good, but it was very wet. He said he had not suffered from his work. He lived 2 miles from the mine, and took a crust underground. He would have his dinner when back home. He had attended evening school for 3d per week, but the teacher had gone to prison for debt. He would like to attend again, but sometimes had to till potatoes for his father.

No. 80 Joseph Roberts (14 years): East Wheal Rose

Joseph had worked for 3 years at surface, and 6 months underground. He worked from 7 am. to 3 pm. wheeling rock for 30 fathoms, from a driving end. It was dry, but after 3 or 4 hours the air would become dead so that he couldn't draw breath. He spat black stuff, sometimes with a cough. He would take a pasty down the mine, but there was no water. He sometimes become very thirsty.

No. 81 Edward Mitchell (16 years): East Wheal Rose

Edward had worked underground at Cornubian (and other mines) for 3 or 4 years. He was currently wheeling ore at the 20 fathom level. He would start work at 8 am., and take a pasty (with pork in it) for dinner. There was no water provided, but he was not thirsty. He had not been able to continue with evening classes as his father was in decline, instead he had to tend their land. (The surgeon noted a hoarse voice, and a predisposition to phthisis).

No. 82 Thomas Chapman (15 years): East Wheal Rose

Thomas only worked 2 or 3 months at surface before going underground at 13, where he was wheeling ore. He was working at 30 fathoms, with no work at night. His hours were 8 am. to 2 pm. He would take dinner down with him, but was not given water to drink. The air was good where he worked, and although he had no difficulty breathing, he sometimes would spit a little.

No. 90 William Trethewy (13 years): Consolidated Mines

William had been working at the mine for 3-4 years at surface, either wheeling ore-stuff or jigging. He considered both of these tasks the hardest at surface. He remarked that only two boys, as well as himself, could jig. The only time they had been jigging all night (a few days previously) the boys had all caught cold. He experienced pains in his arms and legs which stopped when he went to bed. For a week or two in every month he worked from 6 am. to 8 pm., and was given a little extra pay. His wages were 12s per month. Recently he had gone underground for a month or two; turning the borer. He was living 1 mile away from the mine, and would take a potato hoggan for lunch. He only went to day school as a small child, but was currently going to Sunday School.

No. 91 Elisha Morcom (13 years): Consolidated Mines

Elisha had been working at the mine for 4 years and was now jigging or wheeling ore-stuff. He had been ill for a month or two in that time. His wages were 10s 6d per month. He had recently been off work due to an injury where a boy had thrown a stone at him. He was living 2 miles away, and would get up at 4 am. He worked until 5.30 pm. on Saturdays. He would take a potato hoggan for dinner. He had previously attended day school.

No. 92 Richard Jeffrey (9 years): Consolidated Mines

Richard had been working for 8 months at the picking tables. Some days he would stay until 8 pm. and his wages were 6s per month. He would be tired at the end of the day, and his hands became sore, especially when working at the 'shambles' (waste heaps). He was living 2.5 miles away. His father died of cholera in Mexico, and there were 3 other children; 2 working at the mine and 1 dressmaker. He had never been to school.

No. 101 Harry Thomas (10 years): Charlestown Mines
Harry had been serving the buddles for 12 days. He finds it 'rather hard as yet'. He had been to day school but was now attending Sunday School.

No. 102 William Rowett (13 years): Charlestown Mines
William had been serving the buddles for 4 years. He normally worked from 7 am. to 5.30 pm. Once or twice a month he worked 'as long as we can see' followed by I hour for supper. He then continued to work by candlelight until 12 (with another hour break) and through to 2 pm. the following day. He was paid 'a day and a half' for this. Of his 9 siblings, 6 were at the mine. He had been to day school for 18 months, and then Sunday School until 18 months ago, but he had forgotten what he had learnt. He often worked with his father at home. He had kept quite healthy.

No. 105 Jacob Waters (17 years): Fowey Consols
Jacob went to work at the mines at 12, working at the stamps and then for 2 years jigging. He had now been underground for 16 months, currently driving a level; turning or beating the borer. He usually worked from 6 am. to 2 pm., but sometimes worked a double shift. They were blasting 3-4 times per day, when the air was full of smoke, the air being poor where he worked anyway. He felt pains in the head after working some time, which continued after he reached surface. He would eat his pasty where the air was better. He was coughing black stuff each morning, and sometimes had chest pains. He wasn't generally given water underground, and would sweat a great deal and become very thirsty. The changing room was cold; in winter sometimes his shoes were frozen in the chest. He knew of boys 'falling away' in the mine, and his father had his leg broken by falling timber. He had attended day school before entering the mine, and Sunday School for 18 months. He was now at evening school, paying 3d per week (more if a candle was supplied).

No. 106 William Blewett (16 years): Fowey Consols
William had worked at surface from 7 years, and first went underground 'blowing air' when he was 9, working a few months at a time. Sometimes the air was so bad he was sick. At 11 he worked there full time, and before he was 12 had joined his father's tribute team. He was now beating the borer. Much of the time he had been working in poor air, causing him to cough black stuff, and have difficulty climbing the ladders. He had only once worked a double shift. Had been to day school for 1 year, and to Sunday School since.

No. 107 John Collins (14 years): Fowey Consols
John had worked 3 years at surface, and then 7 months underground at the 'blowing machine', on the night shift. He found this hard, giving him headaches and causing lack of appetite at work, and difficulty climbing the ladders. He ate well when he arrived home. In the previous week he worked a double shift to replace a boy who had a serious accident.

He took his own water below ground. His father died 9 years previously, and he had 3 siblings, all working at the mine. He had been to several day schools and Sunday School, but had not been for 9 months 'for want of clothes'. He had forgotten what he had learnt. Once home he collected water and helped in the garden.

No. 108 John Rundel (14 years): Fowey Consols
John began buddling and trucking at 8 yrs, and was often very wet. For 2 years he had been at the blowing machine or hauling tackle at 120 fathoms. He works different shifts on rotation. The air was very bad, he was unable to eat properly, and found it hard to climb the ladders. His father had died, and his 2 brothers were at the mine. He had been to day school for over 3 years and was now going to Sunday School, but had forgotten much of what he had learnt.

No. 109 William Cullis (17 years): Fowey Consols
William began work at the crushers at 12 years, where he had suffered stomach problems and shortness of breath, so that he had been laid up 3 times. About 4 times in 6 months he had worked from 7 am. to 5 am. the following day. He had been jigging for 3 years, and was now healthier, although sometimes he had back ache. He had been to day school for 2 years and then Sunday school until 2 years ago, but he had forgotten much of what he had learnt.

No. 110 John Tillum (14 years): Fowey Consols
John had been working underground at the blowing machine for 4 years. He rarely worked a double shift. At the 170 fathom level it was very hot, and he had been hoarse for about 3 weeks. He was able to eat his pasty below ground. His father was a miner, and he had 5 younger siblings. He went to day school, and continues at Sunday School but has forgotten some of what he learnt.

No. 111 John Spargoe (11 years): Fowey Consols
John had been jigging for 2 years, and finds his back only aches a little. He was paid by the task once or twice per week, when he would finish by 2 or 3 pm. He would then work overtime 'for himself'. He had never worked at night. He had been to day school before starting at the mine, and now goes to Sunday School.

No. 114 Absalom George (13 years): Fowey Consols
Absalom had worked at surface for 2 years. He was then at the blowing machine for 2 weeks, where the air was so bad he was laid up. In the last year he had worked for his father and was paid as 'part of a man'. He often carried tools up the ladders, making him 'pant a good deal', and he spat black stuff after coming to surface. He preferred underground to surface work, as the hours were shorter. He never worked nights or double shifts, and after work he helped on his father's farm. Of his 6 siblings, 4 were at the mine. He went to day school for 4 years, and was continuing at Sunday School.

Bibliography

General Reading

Hamilton Jenkin, A. K. *The Cornish Miner* (Allen & Unwin, 1948)

Kinnaird Commission 1864; *Epitome of Evidence to Lord Kinnaird's Commission Appointed to Inquire into the Condition of All Mines in Great Britain ... with Reference to the Heath and Safety of Such Persons Employed in Such Mines*

Mayers, Lynne: *Balmaidens* (Hypatia Trust, 2004)

Royal Commission 1842; *The Employment of Children and Young People in the Mines of Cornwall and Devonshire, and on the State, Condition and Treatment of Such Children and Young Persons*

Cornwall Federation of Women's Institutes; *Troon Scrapbook, Women and Girls on the Mines and Tin Streams* 1952 (Camborne School of Mines Library)

Chapter 2. Bal Boys

Harris, J.; *Autobiography of a Cornish Miner* (1882)

Drew, Jacob Halls; *Samuel Drew, The Self-Taught Cornishman* (Ward & Co., 1861)

Chapter 4. At the Clay Works

Barton, Rita. M; *The Cornish China Clay Industry* (Bradford Barton, 1966)

Varcoe, Philip; *China Clay, the Early Years* (Francis Antony, 1978)

Chapter 5. Slate Dressers and Packers

Jenkin, John. *Delabole Slate Quarry; a Sketch by a Workman on the Quarry* (Launceston, 1888)

Chapter 6. Smelters, Foundries and Sampling Offices

Barton, D. B. *A History of Copper Mining in Cornwall and Devon* (Truro Bookshop, 1961)

Guthrie, A. *Cornwall in the Age of Steam* (Tabb House, 1994)

Chapter 7. At the Explosives Works

Earl, Bryan; *Cornish Explosives* (Trevithick Society, 1978)

Crocker, Glenys; *The Gunpowder Industry* (Shire, 2002)

Chapter 8. Women Traders and Managers

Barton, Rita. M. *The Cornish China Clay Industry* (Bradford Barton, 1966)

Greeves, Tom. "Women, Tinworks and Mines" *Dartmoor Magazine* No. 83 (Summer 2006) p. 8-10

Palmer, June. *Truro in the 18th Century* (1990)

Website Links

For other mining related websites see our links page on

www.balmaiden.co.uk

Mining Industries Index

Bold numbers refer to Illustrations

Index

Bold numbers refer to Illustrations